New Dimensions

INTERMEDIATE
STUDENT'S BOOK

Robert O'Neill
and **Pat Mugglestone**

Larry Anger

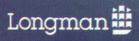

**New Dimensions Intermediate,
Student's Book**

Copyright © 1993 by Longman Publishing Group

All rights reserved.
No part of this publication may be reproduced,
stored in a retrieval system, or transmitted
in any form or by any means, electronic, mechanical,
photocopying, recording, or otherwise,
without the prior permission of the publisher.

Longman, 10 Bank Street, White Plains, N.Y. 10606

Associated companies:
Longman Group UK Ltd., London
Longman Cheshire Pty., Melbourne
Longman Paul Pty., Auckland
Copp Clark Pitman, Toronto

Distributed in the United Kingdom by Longman Group UK Ltd.,
Longman House, Burnt Mill, Harlow, Essex CM20 2JE, England
and by associated companies, branches, and representatives
throughout the world.

ISBN: 0-8013-0459-8

1 2 3 4 5 6 7 8 9 10 – DO – 9695949392

ACKNOWLEDGEMENTS

We are grateful to the following for permission to reproduce
copyright material:

John Murray (Publishers) Ltd. for an adapted extract from *A
Private View* by Beryl Cook; the author, R. O'Neill for extracts
from *Brunswick Messenger* by Art Wellington; Martin Secker &
Warburg Ltd. for an extract from *The Great Extinction* by Michael
Allaby and James Lovelock.

We are grateful to the following for their permission to reproduce
copyright photographs:

Ace Photo Agency for page 37 (k). AGE Fotostock for pages 37 (c, e
and f), 88 and 91. Alpha Photographic Press Agency for pages 23 (c
and f). Aquarius Library for page 19 (top). Camera Press Limited
for pages 30, 37 (d and g). Colorific/Carl Purcell for page 98 (right).
Company/Martin Brading for page 23 (d). Beryl Cook for pages 45,
106. Faberge Incorporated for page 23 (a). The Ronald Grant
Archive for page 99. Hulton-Deutsch for page 27. The Hutchison
Library for page 23 (h). The Image Bank for pages 23 (b) and 37 (a).
Impact Photos for page 37 (j). The Kobal Collection for page 100.
Longman's Photographic Unit for page 68. Magnum/A. Venzago for
page 26. Nature Photographers/R.S. Daniell for page 85.
Picturepoint for page 23 (g). Popperfoto for page 55. Positive
Images/Jerry Howard for page 120. Rex Features for page 19
(bottom). Spectrum Colour Library for page 37 (b, h and i). Tony
Stone Worldwide for page 87,/Click Chicago Limited/Ben
Nakayama for page 98 (left). The Telegraph Colour Library Limited
for page 47. Transworld Feature Syndicate/Scope Features for page
23 (e). Courtesy, The Henry Francis du Pont Winterthur Museum
for page 124.

CONTENTS

Unit 1 ▼ A TRIP TO NEW YORK page 1

1 Reading, Thinking, and Listening 1
Deducing meaning ● Listening to find out which conversation is different

2 Language Study 3
I like and *I'd like* ● The Present Perfect Progressive ● Contrast of the Present Perfect Progressive with the Present Progressive and the Simple Past ● Stress and intonation: It's expensive. Yes, but *how* expensive?

3 Reading and Discussion 5
Comparing three types of text

4 Language Study 6
Verbs + *do*, *to do*, and *doing* ● Prepositions + *-ing* ● The future with the Present Progressive ● Words and sounds: n**or**th, th**ough**t, f**oo**d, d**ea**d, d**ay**s

5 Listening and Writing 8
Comparing a picture with recorded information ● Writing a postcard

Unit 2 ▼ IT'S BEEN A LONG TIME 9

1 Reading and Thinking 9
Finding differences between a story and a picture

2 Language Study 10
Using tag questions to show interest ● Ways to keep conversations going ● *Will you/could you...* ● Making comparisons with *like*

3 Reading and Thinking 12
A letter to a friend ● Figuring out relationships

4 Language Study 13
Contrast of the Simple Past and the Present Perfect ● Separable and inseparable two-word verbs ● Words and sounds: h**ear**d—h**ear**, w**eigh**t—h**eigh**t, **ch**at—**ch**ampagne, appointm**ent**—s**ent**

5 Listening, Discussion, and Writing 15
Family relationships ● Writing a short biography

Language Summary for Unit 1 17
Language Summary for Unit 2 18

Unit 3 ▼ A MODERN LEGEND 19

1 Listening, Reading, and Discussion 19
James Dean ● Words and sounds: He *lives*, Their *lives*; He *leads* an exciting life, It's made of *lead*

2 Language Study 21
Contrast of the Past Progressive and the Simple Past ● Noun forms of verbs (*die*, *death*) ● Stress and intonation: I've seen that movie. Oh, *have* you?—Did you like it? Yes, *did you?* ● Words and sounds: s**igh**t—h**eigh**t, j**ea**ns—pl**ea**sure, color—m**ore**, **lion**—mil**lion**

3 Description 23
Describing people

4 Language Study 24
Physical and personal characteristics ● Idioms with parts of the body (*Keep your fingers crossed.*)

5 Reading, Listening, and Writing 26
An article about a famous person ● Talking and writing about a famous person

Unit 4 ▼ A DIFFERENT WORLD 27

1 Reading and Discussion 27
A different way of life

2 Language Study 29
The past with *used to* ● Words and sounds: **use**, **used to** ● Reflexive (*themselves*) and reciprocal (*each other*) pronouns ● *A little* and *a few*

3 Reading and Discussion 31
Changes in the way we live

4 Language Study 32
Like and *prefer* ● *more/less/fewer ... than* ● Words and sounds: hous**es**—cloth**es**, cloth—clothes

5 Listening and Writing 34
Changes in people's lives ● Writing about yourself

Language Summary for Unit 3 35
Language Summary for Unit 4 36

Unit 5 WOULD YOU EAT IT? 37

1 Reading, Listening, and Discussion 37
Questions about food • Descriptions of food

2 Language Study 39
The passive voice (*are eaten, were discovered*) • Ways to cook food: *fry, bake, broil* • Words and sounds: p**ea**s—br**ea**d—st**ea**k, b**ee**n—b**ee**f, pi**zz**a—fi**sh**

3 Reading and Thinking 41
Personal tastes

4 Language Study 42
Adjectives ending in *-ed* (*disgusted*) and *-ing* (*disgusting*) • *Would rather* and *would prefer* • *I'd rather . . . than . . .* • *Make* vs. *do*

5 Thinking and Writing 44
Writing a letter to a friend

Unit 6 WOULD YOU DO THIS? 45

1 Reading, Listening, and Discussion 45
Comparing an artist's painting with reality • Talking about different kinds of work

2 Language Study 47
Contrast of the Past Perfect and the Simple Past • The meaning of *'d* (*would* or *had*) • Words and sounds: (de**b**t—trou**b**le, **k**nee—**k**ick, li**gh**t—tou**gh**, **h**ouse—**h**our • Stress: What do **you** want? What **do** you want? **What** do you want?

3 Reading and Thinking 49
Employment ads • Jobs and Qualifications

4 Language Study 50
Impersonal *they* • The causative (*I had the TV repaired.*) • Words relating to money: *earn—win, lend—borrow* • Words relating to work: *profession, staff, retire*

5 Writing and Listening 52
Writing a letter to apply for a job • 20 Questions

Language Summary for Unit 5 53
Language Summary for Unit 6 54

Unit 7 ARE THEY CRAZY OR AM I? 55

1 Reading and Thinking 55
Albert Einstein

2 Language Study 56
Words that describe intelligence: *bright, brilliant, sharp, slow* • Words and sounds: **th**ick, **s**ick • The definite article • Adverbs (*always*) and expressions of frequency (*once in a while*)

3 Reading, Listening, and Discussion 58
Identifying the speakers • Listening for further information • Stress and intonation: Is this **your** book? No. I think it's **yours**.

4 Language Study 59
Relative clauses with *who, which,* and *that* • The superlative of adjectives • Nouns ending in *-er* (*murderer*), *-or* (*director*), and *-ist* (*scientist*) • *Always* to show annoyance (*You're always criticizing me.*) • Words and sounds: **ch**ange—**ch**ampagne, **ch**oose—**sh**oes

5 Thinking, Listening, and Writing 61
Questionnaire: Are you introverted or extroverted? • Writing about the kind of people you like to spend time with

Unit 8 SUNDAY IN THE PARK 63

1 Reading, Thinking, and Listening 63
Figuring out who said what

2 Language Study 65
The Conditional in present hypothetical situations (*I would . . . if . . .*) • Words and sounds: s**ou**nd—**ou**ght, b**u**sy—**u**se, personal—personality) • Stress and intonation: We won't be alive 200 years from now, **will we**?)

3 Reading, Thinking, and Listening 67
Letters to an advice column

4 Language Study 68
Should and *ought to* • Words that describe attitudes and feelings: *be crazy about, be furious, envy*

5 Discussion and Writing 70
Problems between parents and children • Writing a letter to an advice column

Language Summary for Unit 7 71

Language Summary for Unit 8 72

Unit 9 ▼ NEWS FROM THE FUTURE 73

1 Reading and Thinking 73
News reports from the future

2 Language Study 75
Can and *be able to* • Contrast of *can* and *will be able to* • *Unless* and *if* • Words and sounds: oper**a**te—oper**a**tion

3 Reading and Discussion 77
A graph about average life expectancy • Historical changes

4 Language Study 78
The Conditional in possible (*What will happen if . . . ?*) and hypothetical (*What would happen if . . . ?*) situations • Contrast of the Simple Future and the Future Progressive • Words and sounds: expl**a**in—explan**a**tion, **a**llergy—all**e**rgic

5 Reading, Listening, and Writing 80
Reading about the future of two young people • Writing about your life ten years from now

Unit 10 ▼ A THREATENED PLANET 81

1 Reading, Thinking, and Listening 81
Dinosaurs and the Earth

2 Language Study 83
Might (may) vs. *could* vs. *should (ought to)* • Past modals: *might (may) have done* and *could have done* • Words, sounds, and stress: **his**tory—hist**o**ric, **cata**strophe, cata**stroph**ic • Noun forms of verbs: *explode, explosion*

3 Reading, Listening, and Discussion 85
Animals that are becoming extinct • Guessing the name of a mystery animal

4 Language Study 86
Reason, *cause*, and *purpose* • Expressing purpose with *for, (in order) to,* and *so (that)*

5 Writing 88
Writing about a city, its problems, and possible solutions

Language Summary for Unit 9 89

Language Summary for Unit 10 90

UNIT 1 A Trip to New York

1 READING

A. Reading

Look at the passengers and read their conversations. Don't worry about the missing words. Then answer these questions.

1. What are the different passengers talking about?
2. Do you think any of the passengers are related?

1
How high are we flying, Dad?
   Very high.
But how high?
   I don't know.
How do you ¹............ we're flying very high, then?

2 Excuse me. Are you feeling all right?
   No, actually, I'm not. Why?
You've got some strange red spots on your face. I just ²............ them.

3
Have you read this?
   Yes, of course I ³............ Don't worry about it.
But just look at what he says.
   Forget it. Everybody else thought you were wonderful. Now, about this party they're giving for you tomorrow night . . .

4
Do you like doing that kind of thing?
   No, not really.
Well, why do you do it, then?
   It pays ⁴............ And I have a family to support.

2 LANGUAGE STUDY

A. *I like* and *I'd like*

1. What is the difference between sentences 1 and 2, and between sentences 3 and 4?

1. I like living there.
2. I'd like to live there.
3. Do you like flying?
4. Would you like to fly?

Which sentence above means:

a. Do you want to fly?
b. Do you ever fly when you travel and do you like it?
c. I live there and I like it.
d. I don't live there, but I want to.

2. Find as many answers as possible for each question.

1. Would you like to go to the movies?
2. Do you like going to the movies?
3. Do you like getting up early?
4. Would you like to visit New York?
5. Would you like to come to my party?
6. Do you like going to parties?

3. Complete the questions with the correct form of *like* or *would like*. Supply answers like the ones in Exercise 2.

1. A: .... you .... to fly to New York with me next week?
   B: .... I have a lot to do here.
2. A: .... you .... living in Los Angeles?
   B: .... We don't like the traffic.
3. A: .... he .... working in the United States?
   B: .... He thinks it's very exciting.
4. A: .... you .... to go to a movie tonight?
   B: .... But I want to do my homework first.

4. On a personal level. Work in a group and find out about your classmates. Take notes.

1. Make a list of things your group likes doing on weekends.
2. Find out what each person would like to do next weekend.

B. The Present Perfect Progressive (*I've been living*)

1. Study these sentences.

1. She's been living in Los Angeles for ten years. (She moved to Los Angeles ten years ago. She's living there now.)
2. We've been flying for two hours. (The plane took off two hours ago. We're still flying.)
3. I haven't been doing much since I retired. (I retired. I'm not doing much now.)

Now complete these sentences with *'s/hasn't been* or *'ve/haven't been*.

4. The passengers like each other. They .... talking since the plane took off.
5. I'm sorry I'm late. I hope you .... waiting for very long.
6. She's an anthropologist. She .... studying different groups of people around the world.

2. Use the information to make a single statement. Use *for* or *since* in your statement.

Example She came to work four hours ago.
She's still working.
She's been working for four hours.

1. She started studying English last year. She's still studying.
2. They moved to New York in August. They're living there now.
3. We arrived at the hotel three days ago. We're staying there now.
4. I came to the theater at seven o'clock to meet my wife. I'm still waiting for her.
5. My brother stopped doing a lot of things when he broke his leg. He's still not doing much.

3. On a personal level. Tell your classmates about yourself.

1. Say how long you've been living here.
2. Say how long you've been studying English.
3. Tell them how long you've been taking English classes at this school.
4. Tell them when you started this particular course.

C. The Present Perfect Progressive (*I have been staying*), the Present Progressive (*I am staying*), and the Simple Past (*I stayed*)

1. Study these three questions.

1. How long are you staying there?
2. How long have you been staying there?
3. How long did you stay there?

Now find the right answer (a, b, or c) to the questions above.

a. Only for a few days. Then I went to another hotel.
b. Only for a few days. Since last Friday, in fact.
c. Only for a few days. Until next Friday, in fact.

2. Complete these sentences with the correct form of the verb in parentheses.

1. Where have you been? I (*wait*) for you for over an hour!
2. I stood outside the theater and (*wait*) for you for over an hour yesterday!
3. A: How long (*you stay*) in New York?
   B: At least a week.
4. I (*study*) English for a long time now.
5. I (*learn*) Greek and Latin when I was in school, but I don't think they're very useful.
6. I also (*study*) Spanish when I was younger, but I still can't speak it.
7. You (*smoke*) again! I can smell it on your clothes!
8. The director is in New York at the moment. She (*stay*) there until the 12th.
9. James Dean (*make*) only three movies in Hollywood before he was killed.
10. When was the last time you (*go*) to a movie?
11. I (*live*) alone for several years now, and I'm still enjoying my independence.
12. I (*live*) by myself once, but I didn't enjoy it.

D. Pronunciation: Stress and Intonation

1. Listen to these conversations. Then read them aloud. Pay special attention to the words in *italics*.

1. A: How high are we flying?
   B: Very high.
   A: Yes, but *how high*?
   B: I don't know.
2. A: How far is it to New York?
   B: It's pretty far.
   A: Yes, but *how far*?
   B: About 3,000 miles.

2. Supply the missing words in these conversations. Then read them aloud and practice the correct stress.

1. A: How much is a ticket to New York?
   B: Oh, it's very expensive.
   A: Well, ...?
   B: About $500.
2. A: How far is it to the airport?
   B: It's not far.
   A: Yes, but ....?
   B: I don't know exactly.
3. A: When will you be able to fix my car?
   B: Soon.
   A: Yes, but ....?
   B: As soon as I have time.
4. A: Did I make many mistakes?
   B: No, not many.
   A: But ....?
   B: I can't remember exactly. One or two.
5. A: How was the movie?
   B: It was long.
   A: Really? ....?
   B: About three hours.

Now listen to all these conversations. Was your stress and intonation the same?

▶ UNIT 1

3 READING AND DISCUSSION

▼ A. Reading

Study the three texts and answer these questions.

1. One is a diary entry. What are the other two?
2. Where would you find a text like "A Dead Film About a Dead Actor"?

A Dead Film About a Dead Actor

The third and last of the new films to open this week is *Dean*. It is about the actor of the same name and stars Simon Farnham in the title role. Farnham is an unknown young actor, and if this is an example of his acting talent, it would obviously be better if he remained that way. It is true that he looks like the real Dean. However, he totally lacks his magnetism and magic. All that can be said in favor of the movie itself is that it is at least accurate as a record of Dean's short life and his obsession with death and fast cars. Dean, who died tragically in 1955 after making only three movies, was a lion of the screen. Farnham, unfortunately, is no comparison.

—SDAY

Mr. and Mrs. Thomas Andrews
request the honor of your presence at the
marriage of their daughter
Kimberly Ann Andrews
to
William James Berenson
Saturday, the sixteenth of October at 2 PM
St. Peter's Church
1224 Ventura Boulevard
Los Angeles, California 90047

FRIDAY

Dear Diary,

Dad and I have been here for a week now, but I still haven't seen as much of the city as I'd like to. Dad spends most of the day in this apartment, talking to Aunt Laura. Then, when Uncle Roger comes back home, he and Dad sit in front of the TV, watching football or something like that. Ugh!

I've been on the subway a few times, and tomorrow we're all going to Chinatown. I'd also like to go to some of the museums, but as usual Dad just isn't interested. If only he'd let me go out alone! I'm looking forward to going to Princeton and seeing where Einstein used to live. It isn't very far away, and before we left Los Angeles, Dad promised to take me there. I just hope he hasn't forgotten!

NOTES

▼ B. Discussion

1. Give your opinion. Do your classmates agree?

1. Why do you think the newspaper article is called "A Dead Film About a Dead Actor"?
2. Explain what you think "a lion of the screen" is.
3. Would you go to see the movie after reading this review? Why or why not?
4. Who sent the wedding announcement?
5. Pretend you are talking to some people who know Kim Andrews. They haven't seen the wedding announcement. How would you give them the information? Use your own words.
6. Think about the diary entry. Which person on the plane wrote this? What is the writer's father like?

2. On a Personal Level

1. Imagine that you keep a diary. What are some of the things you would write about last week?
2. Imagine you are in New York now. What would you like to do?

4 LANGUAGE STUDY

A. Verb + *do*, *to do*, or *doing*

1. Can you guess the right form? Complete these sentences with either *do*, *to do*, or *doing*.

1. You promised .... it.
2. What do you enjoy .... in the evening?
3. What would you like .... now?
4. My parents won't let me .... anything alone.
5. They make me .... all sorts of things I don't want to do.
6. I hate .... this kind of thing.
7. What time will you finish .... your homework?
8. Will you help me .... the dishes after dinner?

2. Use the chart below to check your answers to Exercise 1.

1. In which sentence in Exercise 1 can you use either *to do* or *doing*?
2. In which sentence can you use either *do* or *to do*?

Verb + *do*	Verb + *to do*	Verb + *doing*	Verb + *to do* or *doing*
let make help (or *to do*)	decide forget hope need plan promise want would like	discuss enjoy finish keep practice quit suggest avoid	begin continue hate love like prefer start stop try

3. Study the use of *stop*. What is the difference in the meaning of these sentences?

1. I stopped seeing her after our fight.
2. I stopped to see her after our fight.

Which one means:

a. I haven't seen her since our fight.
b. We had a fight, so I went to see her.

4. Complete these sentences with the correct form of the verb in parentheses.

1. Do you practice (*speak*) English every day?
2. They decided (*eat*) dinner in Chinatown.
3. Stop (*make*) all that noise! I want (*study*).
4. When do you plan (*have*) the wedding?
5. She won't let her brother (*use*) her cassettes.
6. I love (*go*) to weddings.
7. We hope (*visit*) New York soon.
8. I stopped (*visit*) my grandmother, but she wasn't home.
9. All right, class. Please begin (*read*) page 8.
10. His mother makes him (*finish*) his homework before he watches TV.

B. Prepositions + *doing*

1. Study these sentences. Notice the prepositions and the words that follow them.

1. Are you ever bored with doing the same thing every day?
2. I'm excited about doing this.
3. I'm good at doing math problems.
4. What are you thinking of doing for your birthday?

Now refer to the list and complete these sentences.

be bored with	be tired of
be excited about	look forward to
be good at	think about/of
be interested in	

5. Is he interested .... doing this kind of work?
6. They were tired .... doing their homework.
7. I'm looking forward .... doing it.
8. What are you thinking .... doing tonight?

2. Complete these sentences with the correct forms of the verbs in parentheses.

1. I'm looking forward to (*go*) to Princeton and (*see*) where Einstein used to live.
2. She's thinking about (*fly*) to New York. She likes (*visit*) different cities.
3. Are you good at (*write*) letters in English? I want (*write*) to a friend in the United States.
4. We aren't really interested in (*do*) this. In fact, we hate (*do*) things like this.
5. I'm bored with (*study*). I think I'll stop (*do*) this exercise right now.

3. On a personal level. Practice this conversation with a partner.

A: What do you enjoy doing in your free time?
B: I enjoy/like .... And I'm pretty good at ...., so I .... a lot. What about you?
A: Well, I really like ...., and I'm interested in ....

▶ C. The Future with the Present Progressive (*I'm having*)

1. Are these three sentences the same or different in meaning?

1. I have an appointment in Chinatown tomorrow, so I'm going to have lunch there.
2. I have an appointment in Chinatown tomorrow, so I'll have lunch there.
3. I have an appointment in Chinatown tomorrow, so I'm having lunch there.

It is often possible to use the Present Progressive (*be having*) rather than *be going to have* or *will have* without changing the meaning—especially if you are talking about things people plan or intend to do.

2. Complete these sentences with the Present Progressive (*be . . .ing*) if possible. If not, use *be going to . . .* or *will*.

1. We (*fly*) to New York next week.
2. I (*see*) the boss tomorrow.
3. Do you think we (*have*) better weather soon?
4. Mary (*have*) a baby next month.
5. I don't know when we (*leave*).
6. I (*lose*) my job if I'm late again.

In which two sentences did you have to use *be going to . . .* or *will*? Were these sentences about things people plan or intend to do? Does this tell you anything about when you can't use *be . . .ing*?

3. Change this conversation. Use the Present Progressive (*be . . .ing*) for the future (*be going to . . ./will*) when it is possible.

A: I wonder if it's going to rain next weekend.
B: Why?
A: Because I'm going to go to Los Angeles on Saturday.
B: Oh? How long are you going to stay?
A: Until Sunday. I have some friends there, and they're going to have a party.
B: How are you going to get there?
A: I'm going to drive.
B: Could I come with you? I'm going to meet some friends in L.A. too.
A: Sure. But another friend is going to come, so there won't be much room.

4. On a personal level. You want to have a party either next Friday or Saturday night. You don't know which day is better because you don't know who in your group already has plans.

1. Find out if your classmates are doing anything next Friday night.
2. Find out what they are doing next Saturday night.

Which day would be better for the party? Why?

▶ D. Pronunciation: Words and Sounds

Listen to these words. Then say them aloud. Pay special attention to the letters in bold. Which word in each group has a different sound?

1. Y**or**k b**or**n n**or**th hist**or**y
2. w**ou**ld c**ou**ld sh**ou**ld th**ou**ght
3. ar**ou**nd s**ou**nd t**ow**n th**ou**ght
4. l**oo**k g**oo**d w**ou**ld f**oo**d
5. f**oo**d m**oo**n sch**oo**l f**oo**t
6. d**ea**d s**ai**d r**e**d D**ea**n
7. D**ea**n scr**ee**n **e**vening st**ea**k
8. d**ay** d**ay**s s**ay** s**ay**s

5 LISTENING AND WRITING

A. Listening

1. 🔊 Close your eyes and listen to the conversation at least once. As you listen, form a picture in your mind of the people who are talking and where they are.

2. After you listen to the conversation, answer these questions.

1. When you listened, how many people did you think there were?
2. Where did you think the people were?
3. Who did you think each person was?
4. What did you think was going to happen at the end?

3. Now compare the picture in your mind with the picture on this page. How are they different?

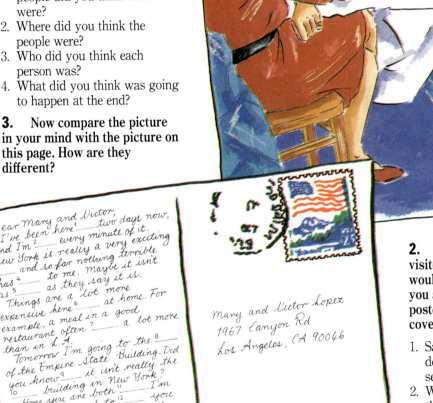

Dear Mary and Victor,
I've been here¹ ___ two days now, and I'm² ___ every minute of it. New York is really a very exciting ³ ___ and so far nothing terrible has⁴ ___ to me. Maybe it isn't as⁵ ___ as they say it is.
Things are a lot more expensive here⁶ ___ at home. For example, a meal in a good restaurant often⁷ ___ a lot more than in L.A.
Tomorrow I'm going to the⁸ ___ of the Empire State Building. Did you know⁹ ___ it isn't really the ¹⁰ ___ building in New York?
Hope you are both¹¹ ___. I'm looking forward to¹² ___ you and¹³ ___ you all about it when I get¹⁴ ___.
Love, Kim

Mary and Victor Lopez
1967 Canyon Rd
Los Angeles, CA 90046

2. Think of a place you have visited recently or that you would like to visit soon. Imagine you are there now and write a postcard to a friend. Be sure to cover all these points.

1. Say where you are and describe something you have seen or done.
2. What are your impressions of this place?
3. What do you like or dislike about it?
4. What are you looking forward to doing?
5. Think of a few words to write at the end of the postcard.

B. Writing

1. This is a postcard from someone who was on the flight to New York. Here are five of the missing words. Where do they belong?

a. place   b. dangerous   c. top   d. tallest   e. telling

What are the other nine missing words?

UNIT 2 It's Been a Long Time

1 READING AND THINKING

A. Reading

Read the text. Compare the picture carefully with the scene the text describes.

1. What is different about the man and woman in the picture and the couple described in the text?
2. What do you think the people in the picture might be saying to each other?
3. Can you find any other differences between the picture and the text?

B. Reading and Thinking

Read the text again and answer these questions.

1. What do you think the relationship is between the man and woman in the story?
2. What could have happened in their lives before the story begins?
3. What do you think happened after the couple drank the champagne? For example, did one of them stand up and walk out of the restaurant a few minutes later? Did they start to argue? Or . . . ?

When the tall man came into the restaurant, people looked at him and whispered. He was in his late 40s or early 50s. His dark hair was turning gray and he had a beard. He was dressed casually in a sports coat and open shirt. The head waiter smiled and immediately took him to a table near the window. Another waiter brought him the menu. He looked at it quickly. "I'm expecting someone else, so I'll order later," he said. The waiter nodded and turned to go.

"Just a second. Bring me a bottle of your best champagne and two glasses," the man said.

A few minutes later, a woman in her mid 20s came in. She was wearing a simple but elegant dress under a plain, tan raincoat. She was tall and slim. As soon as he saw her, the man stood up and motioned to her. She walked towards him. They looked at each other silently for a moment.

"It's been a long time," he said and smiled.

"Yes," she answered. She did not smile back.

"Won't you sit down?" he said.

The waiter took her coat and brought her a menu. Then he poured her a glass of champagne.

"Do you like champagne?" he asked.

"Sometimes. It depends," she answered. She paused and drank a little of the pale, sparkling liquid.

"Very nice," she said. The man smiled again, but he seemed rather afraid of her. There was something hard and cold about her, like ice.

2 LANGUAGE STUDY

A. Tag Questions

1. Study these conversations. Notice the words in *italics*.

1. A: It's a nice day, *isn't it*?
   B: Yes, it is. It isn't so cold today, *is it*?
   A: No.
2. A: You haven't been here since 1985, *have you*?
   B: No, I haven't. It has changed a lot, *hasn't it*?
   A: Yes, it has.

Now complete these questions with the words in the box.

will you?   do you?   doesn't he?   can't you?

3. A: You don't know my friend Mike, ...
   B: No, I don't. He goes to your school, ...
   A: Yes.
4. A: You can come to my party, ...
   B: Sure. You won't mind if I bring a friend, ...
   A: Not at all.

Are the speakers in conversations 1–4 asking for confirmation of their statements? Or are they asking for new information?

2. Supply the missing words in these questions.

1. The weather has been awful lately, ... it?
2. It would be nice to take a vacation, ... it?
3. The French Riviera is very popular as a vacation spot, ... it?
4. Your parents are going to Japan next summer, ... they?
5. They should begin planning their trip soon, ... they?
6. You weren't in Mexico last year, ... you?
7. You don't have much money to spend on hotels, ... you?
8. We didn't spend much money last year, ... we?

What answers should you give to the questions above if you want to agree with the speaker?

3. You have just said "Nice day today." Which of the answers below did John give? Which answer did Ann give?

1. Yes.
2. Yes, it is, isn't it?

Which answer suggests that the speaker is interested in keeping the conversation going and wants to talk? Which answer suggests that the speaker isn't interested in talking?

4. Imagine that you are at a party and someone says the things below to you. Give answers that suggest you are interested and want to talk.

1. It's a nice party.
2. The food looks good.
3. Look at that man over there. He doesn't look very happy.
4. The woman near the door looks interesting.
5. The music is so loud I can't hear myself think.

B. Other Ways to Keep the Conversation Going

1. Study these questions.

1. Would you like to go to the movies tonight?
2. Now, do you understand what I just told you?
3. Have you ever been to New York?
4. Could you lend me some money until tomorrow?
5. Do you like living here?
6. Are you hungry?

The answers below help keep the conversation going. Which answer goes with which question? What do you think was said next in each conversation?

a. No, I haven't. But I'm planning a trip next year.
b. Not really. Why? Are you?
c. It depends on what's playing.
d. How much do you need?
e. Well, yes and no. I mean, there are a lot of things I like about it, but there are some things I hate.
f. I think so, but there are a few things I'm still not sure about.

2. On a personal level. Imagine that you are at a party and someone says these things to you. With a partner or in a group, think of answers that help keep the conversation going.

Example   A: Do you like music?
　　　　　　B: I like some kinds of music but not all.
　　　　　　A: What kinds do you like?
　　　　　　B: I like rock the best. What about you?

1. Tell me. Are you interested in sports at all?
2. Do you ever watch television?
3. Do you have any hobbies?
4. Do you enjoy doing exercises like these?

C. Asking People to Do Things

1. Study the sentences and decide who the speaker is talking to. Is it someone:

a. the speaker knows very well, like a close friend?
b. the speaker doesn't know very well and wants to be very polite to?
c. whose job it is to do what the speaker wants?

1. Bring me a bottle of your best champagne.
2. Will you close that window?
3. Sit down.
4. The train station, please. As fast as you can!
5. Could I have some champagne too?
6. Excuse me, but would you mind closing that window?
7. Won't you sit down?
8. I don't want to put you to any trouble, but do you think you could possibly take me to the station?

2. Find two responses for each of the requests in Exercise 1. One response should agree with the request. The other should refuse or make an excuse.

a. Thanks.
b. Yes, sir.
c. I'm sorry. We don't have champagne.
d. No. You've had enough.
e. Sure.
f. I can't. I just painted it.
g. I'm sorry, but I don't like driving fast.
h. No thanks. I've been sitting all day.
i. I'm sorry, I can't. I don't have a car.
j. Thank you.
k. I'd like to, but I can't stay. I have an appointment.
l. Not at all.

3. On a personal level. Decide what you would say in these situations and ask your partner to do the things for you. Your partner will agree or refuse and give an excuse.

1. You work in an office. A co-worker you don't know very well just came in and forgot to close the door.
2. A very good friend at work or at school is about to go for a walk and will pass the post office. You need some stamps and don't have time to get them yourself.
3. It's raining and you have to get home quickly. Someone you don't know very well has a car.
4. You want to use the public telephone. You don't have the right change. You see an older woman walking her dog.

D. Making Comparisons

Complete the sentences with the words in the box.

a movie star	ice	little soldiers
diamonds	a cherry	glass
fire	a puppy	a spring flower

1. There was something hard and cold about her, like ....
2. He is tall, dark, and handsome, like ....
3. The little boy had big, sad eyes, like ....
4. She has a soft, pale beauty, like ....
5. The sunset was red, yellow, and orange, like ....
6. Like ...., the children marched into school for their first class.
7. The stars, like ...., shine in the sky every night.
8. It was very cold and her nose was red, like ....
9. It was a calm night and the ocean was smooth, just like ....

3 READING AND THINKING

A. Reading

1. Here is part of a letter from a visitor to New York. Read it without worrying about the missing words. What do you think the connection is between this letter and the story on page 9?

2. Find the missing words in the letter.

1. Here are five of the ten missing words. Where should they go?
   a. weather   b. mean   c. on
   d. up   e. time

2. What do you think the other five missing words are?

B. Discussion

Give your opinion. Do your classmates agree?

1. Who could Tony be?
2. Why is Jennifer in New York?
3. Where do you think she was when she wrote the letter?
4. Who could "they" be in "They've given me a month to decide"?
5. What impression do you get of Jennifer herself? How old is she? What kind of education does she have? What are some of her goals in life? etc.

The Randolf Hotel
44 West 46th Street
New York, NY 10036

Dear Tony,

I've been here for almost a week now, and I still haven't decided whether to take the job. I just can't make¹ ___ my mind. You² ___ me before I came here that I shouldn't let our relationship get in the way of my decision. Did you really³ ___ that? They've⁴ ___ me a month to decide. We can talk about it when I get back to L.A. next week.

Do you remember Jeff Hemsky? He was one of the guys we knew at college (he has put⁵ ___ a lot of weight since then). Well, I ran into him two days ago. He's a broker with one of the big Wall Street firms now. He thinks I should take the job even if only for a year or so. He says it would be excellent experience.

Fall is a wonderful⁶ ___ to visit New York. The ⁷___ has been pleasant (warm and sunny but not too hot), and the trees have turned the most beautiful colors. The leaves are much brighter and richer⁸ ___ I imagined.

By the way, I had dinner with my father last night. He hasn't changed very much since I last saw him almost ten years ⁹___. We chatted about this and that, but I didn't really feel like¹⁰ ___. You know it's funny, but I never felt very close to him even when he and my mother were married.

4 LANGUAGE STUDY

A. The Simple Past (*I lived*) or the Present Perfect (*I've lived*)

1. Match each of these sentences (1–8) with the phrases (a–h).

1. I've done a lot of sightseeing
2. I did a lot of sightseeing
3. The sun has gone down
4. The sun went down
5. I've been to the Metropolitan Museum
6. I went to the Metropolitan Museum
7. I've lived in New York
8. I lived in New York

a. yesterday and I'm going to do some more today.
b. since I've been here.
c. and it is dark now.
d. and it got very dark.
e. last week and may go again this week.
f. twice this week.
g. for two years and I love it.
h. for two years and then I moved.

2. Complete these sentences with *have ('ve)/haven't* or *has ('s)/hasn't*.

1. I (*not*) .... seen my girlfriend for a week now.
2. She .... gone to New York for a few days.
3. A big company .... offered her a great job there.
4. She (*not*) .... accepted it yet, but I think she will.
5. She .... had a lot of free time in New York.
6. She and a friend .... done a lot of sightseeing.
7. We (*not*) .... talked much since she left Los Angeles.
8. .... she missed me since she left for New York? No, I don't think so.

The verbs below are from sentences 1–8. Complete the chart.

Base Form	Past Participle	Base Form	Past Participle
....	seen	....	had
go	....	do	....
....	offered	....	talked
....	accepted	miss	....

3. Complete these sentences with the Simple Past (*I saw*) or the Present Perfect (*I have seen*).

Examples I (*see*) that film last week.
I saw that film last week.

.... you ever (*see*) that man before?
Have you ever seen that man before?

1. I (*see*) more than a hundred movies this year.
2. I (*see*) more than a hundred movies last year.
3. .... you (*eat*) yet?
4. What .... you (*eat*) last night?
5. What .... you (*do*) yesterday?
6. I (*apply*) for a new job. I hope I get it.
7. I (*apply*) for a new job, but I didn't get it.
8. How much money .... you (*spend*) on food last week?
9. How much .... you (*spend*) on food so far this week?
10. I think we (*do*) this kind of exercise before, but I'm still not sure I understand.

4. On a personal level. Interview a classmate and take notes so you can report to the class. Find out:

1. a. the name of your classmate's best friend.
   b. how long your classmate has known this person.
   c. where your classmate met his or her best friend.
2. a. if your classmate has ever been to (a popular sight or city in your country) before.
   b. how many times your classmate has been there.
   c. how long your classmate stayed the last time he or she was there.

B. Two-Word Verbs

1. Study the words in *italics*. What is different about these words in each pair of sentences?

1. The pilot and the flight attendants *went on* the plane before the passengers did.
2. The lights *went on* a few minutes ago.

3. *Put* those things *on* the table.
4. I've *put on* a lot of weight recently.
5. I *ran into* an old friend yesterday.
6. I *ran into* the street when I heard the explosion.

2.   An important word is missing in each of these sentences. What is it?

1. Please turn .... the lights before you leave.
2. It's dark in here. Turn .... the light, please.
3. I'm trying to give .... smoking.
4. What time do you usually get .... in the morning?
5. Who will look .... the house while you're away?
6. The plane is taking .... in a few minutes.
7. Please fill .... this form.
8. The car has broken .... again.
9. If I don't understand a word, I usually look it .... in my dictionary.
10. Look ....! There's a car coming!
11. I can't go .... studying two-word verbs any longer!
12. No, no! Keep .... it! Don't stop yet!

3.   Here is a list of the two-word verbs in this unit. Study the verbs and check your answers in Exercise 2.

break down	go on (= continue)	run into
fill in/out	keep at	sit down
get back	look after	stand up
get up	look at	take off (a plane)
give up	look out	take off (clothes)
go down	look up	turn on
go on (lights)	put on	turn off

Now complete these sentences with a two-word verb from the list. Be sure to use the correct tense.

1. The plane ...., but the mechanics fixed it.
2. Let's hurry. The plane is going to .... soon.
3. Please .... and fasten your seat belts.
4. The captain has .... the No Smoking sign, so you may smoke now.
5. I don't smoke anymore. I .... cigarettes last year.
6. Look! The sun .... and the sky is turning orange.
7. Have you ever .... a famous movie star in Los Angeles?
8. I can't wear this sweater. I've .... too much weight.

4.   Study these sentences from Exercise 3. There are two ways to say each sentence.

4. The captain has *turned off* the No Smoking sign.
   The captain has *turned* the No Smoking sign *off*.
5. I *gave up* cigarettes last year.
   I *gave* cigarettes *up* last year.
6. I've *put on* too much weight.
   I've *put* too much weight *on*.

You can separate the two-word verbs in these sentences. Say each sentence in a different way.

1. I gave up desserts because I was getting too fat.
2. If students don't know the meanings of new words, they should look up the words in a dictionary.
3. I can't put on these clothes. They're too small.
4. Will you take off that hat, please? It looks terrible.
5. Please turn off the radio.
6. Do you mind if I turn on the TV?

5.   On a personal level. Answer these questions.

1. Do you have a cassette player? Can you tell your partner or group how to use it?
2. Have you ever bought anything from a vending machine, like candy or soda? What did you have to do?

C. Pronunciation

1.   Listen to these words. Then say them aloud. Pay special attention to the letters in bold.

1. b**ear**d   h**er**e   h**ear**   h**ear**d
2. h**ear**d   b**ir**d   h**er**   b**ur**n
3. w**ear**   wh**ere**   **air**   h**air**
4. p**eo**ple   s**ee**m   l**ea**ve   p**i**zza
5. w**ai**t   **eigh**t   w**eigh**t   h**eigh**t
6. b**ough**t   **ough**t   c**augh**t   **though**t
7. **ch**at   **ch**ampagne   **sh**are   **sh**all
8. **e**legant   appointm**e**nt   pl**e**asant   s**e**nt

2.   In some of the word groups above, the sound of the letters in bold is always the same. In which ones? Which groups have a sound that is different from the others?

5 LISTENING, DISCUSSION, AND WRITING

A. Listening

1. Before you listen, read the summaries of what three of these people say about their childhood. There are important differences between these summaries and what the speakers actually say.

Carol Simpson

Mike Lopez

Vicky Chan

George Black

Carol has a good relationship with both her parents. They have helped her, but they have never tried to make her do things she didn't want to do. Although she doesn't live near them, she sees them often and she calls them at least once a week.

Mike didn't leave home until he was 22. He is married now and has a family of his own. He doesn't live very far from his parents and he sees them a lot. His mother helps his wife and they like each other. Mike says he isn't a "typical American" because he wasn't born in the United States. He says that in the United States, young men and women usually leave home as soon as possible and they don't see their parents very often.

Vicky seems to get along better with her mother than with her father. She says that she is going to have a baby soon and that her mother is very happy about it. Vicky also has a brother, but her mother has never put pressure on him to have children. Vicky is unhappy because her father is so uninterested in her and whether she has children or not.

2. 🔲 Listen to each speaker and see if you can find the differences between the summaries above and what the speakers really say.

1. Has any important information been left out of the summaries above or has any information been changed?
2. Give the summaries again in their corrected forms.

3. 🔲 Now listen to the fourth speaker. Then answer these questions.

1. Who does the speaker seem to have a better relationship with, his mother or his father?
2. Which of his parents seems to be in better health?
3. How does he keep in touch with his parents?
4. What kind of things do his parents like doing?

4. Write a short summary (50–60 words) about the fourth speaker's relationship with his parents. These words may help you:

He is closer to .... than ....
His father .... a few years ago.
It isn't easy for him to .... because ....

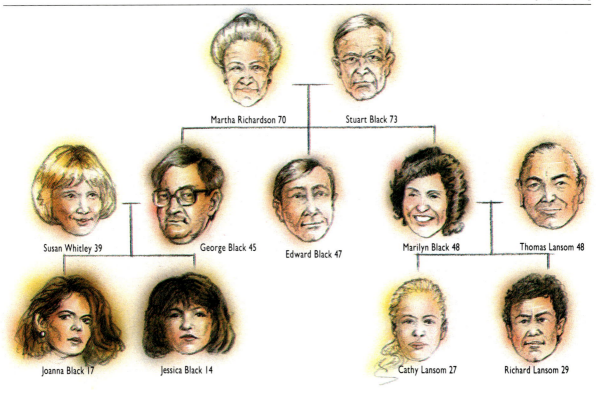

B. Discussion

Study the family tree and try to figure out the relationships of the different people.

1. Answer these questions.

1. Who are Stuart and Martha Black's grandchildren?
2. Does George Black have any nephews or nieces? If so, what are their names?
3. Does anybody have a father-in-law or a mother-in-law?
4. Who has both a brother-in-law and a sister-in-law?
5. Pretend that you are Joanna Black. Look at all the other people in the family. What are their relationships to you?

2. On a personal level. Find out the names of the people in a classmate's family. Do they know the names of their grandparents, uncles, aunts, etc.? What else do they know about them? Do they know their age, date of birth, death, etc.? After you have done this, see if you can draw their family tree.

C. Writing

1. Read this short biography that Vicky Chan wrote.

A SHORT LIFE HISTORY

My grandfather was born in China. He came from a very poor family and was one of seven children. His parents lived on a small farm. He didn't have a very good education. At the age of 17 he left home. First he went to Shanghai and then he went to Hong Kong. He worked as a waiter and then as a cook. When he was 21, he married my grandmother and had four children. My mother was the oldest.

My grandmother died recently, and my grandfather lives alone now. He is almost 80, but he is still very active and interested in everything that is going on. He reads the papers and watches television even though his eyesight is fairly poor.

2. Write a short biography of a relative or a close friend. Include:

- when and where he or she was born.
- information about his or her early childhood and education.
- details about his or her marriage and children.
- information about his or her job and career.
- anything else that is important, for example, interests and hobbies.

LANGUAGE SUMMARY FOR UNIT 1

1. Saying what you like and what you want

Do you like flying?
I like living in the city. I don't like the country.

Would you like to live in New York?
I'd like to live in Los Angeles, but I wouldn't like to live in New York.

2. Describing actions that began in the past and are continuing now

He's been living in Los Angeles for two years.
I haven't been doing much since I retired.

3. Talking about the present and the past

How long are you staying there?
   Only for a few days. Until next Friday, in fact.
How long have you been staying there?
   Only for a few days. Since last Friday, in fact.
How long did you stay there?
   Only for a few days. Then I went to another hotel.

4. Using verbs followed by an infinitive (with or without *to*) or a gerund

Dad promised to take me to Princeton.
What do you enjoy doing in the evening?
My parents won't let me go anywhere alone.
Do you like reading/to read this sort of thing?
Will you help me to do/do the dishes after dinner?
I stopped to see her after our fight. I wanted to apologize.
I stopped seeing her after our fight. I never want to see her again.

5. Using gerunds after prepositions

I'm good at doing math problems.
Is he interested in doing this sort of work?
They were tired of doing their homework.
I'm looking forward to doing it.
What are you thinking about doing tonight?

6. Talking about the future with the Present Progressive, *be going to*, and *will*

I'm having lunch in Chinatown tomorrow. (something you plan or
I'm going to have lunch in intend to do)
Chinatown tomorrow.

Do you think we're going to have (something
better weather soon? you cannot
Do you think we'll have better plan or
weather soon? arrange)

7. Pronunciation: Stress and Intonation

How **high** are we **fly**ing, **Dad**?
   Very high.
But **how high**?
   I **don't know.**

8. Words and Sounds

1. n**o**rth   hist**o**ry
2. w**ou**ld   th**ou**ght
3. ar**ou**nd   t**ow**n   th**ou**ght
4. l**oo**k   w**ou**ld   f**oo**d
5. f**oo**d   f**oo**t
6. d**ea**d   s**ai**d   r**e**d   D**ea**n
7. D**ea**n   scr**ee**n   **eve**ning   st**ea**k
8. d**ay**   d**ay**s   s**ay**   s**ay**s

LANGUAGE SUMMARY FOR UNIT 2

1. Asking for confirmation

It's a nice day, isn't it?
   Yes, it is.
You haven't been here since 1985, have you?
   No, I haven't.

2. Showing interest with tag questions

It's a nice party.
   Yes, it is, isn't it?
The food looks good.
   Yes, it does, doesn't it?
Look at that man over there. He doesn't look very happy.
   No, he doesn't, does he?

3. Keeping the conversation going by asking questions

Do you like music?
   I like some kinds of music but not all. What about you?
Tell me. Are you interested in sports at all? What about you?
   I'm interested in swimming and soccer.
Do you ever watch television?
   Now and then. It depends on what's on. And you?
Do you enjoy doing exercises like these?
   Well, to tell you the truth, no. How do you feel about them?

4. Asking people to do things

Bring me a bottle of your best champagne.
   Yes, sir.
Will you close that window?
   Sure.
Could I have some champagne too?
   No. You've had enough.
Excuse me, but would you mind closing that window?
   Not at all.
Won't you sit down?
   I'd like to, but I can't stay. I have an appointment.

5. Making comparisons

There was something hard and cold about her, like ice.
He is tall, dark, and handsome, like a movie star.
Like little soldiers, the children marched into school for their first class.
The stars, like diamonds, shine in the sky every night.

6. Using the Simple Past and the Present Perfect

I've done a lot of sightseeing since I've been here.
I did a lot of sightseeing yesterday, and I'm going to do some more today.

Have you eaten yet?
What did you eat last night?

How much money have you spent on food so far this week?
How much money did you spend on food last week?

7. Using separable and inseparable two-word verbs

The car has broken down again.
I ran into an old friend yesterday.

The captain has turned off the No Smoking sign, so you may smoke now. (The captain has turned the No Smoking sign off, so you may smoke now.)
I gave up cigarettes last year. (I gave cigarettes up last year.)

8. Pronunciation

These groups have the same vowel sound:
h**ear**d b**ir**d h**er** b**ur**n
w**ear** wh**ere** **air** h**air**
p**eo**ple s**ee**m l**ea**ve p**i**zza
b**ough**t **ough**t c**augh**t th**ough**t

There is one word with a different vowel sound in these groups:
b**ear**d h**ere** h**ear** h**ear**d
w**ai**t **ei**ght w**eigh**t h**eigh**t
el**e**gant appointm**e**nt pl**ea**sant s**e**nt

There is one word with a different consonant sound in this group:
champagne **sh**are **sh**all **ch**at

UNIT 3 A Modern Legend

1 LISTENING, READING, AND DISCUSSION

A. Discussion

Look at the pictures and discuss them with your classmates.

1. What was this person's name?
2. Find out how many people in your class have ever seen any of his movies.
3. Which movies have they seen?
4. Why do you think he is called "A Modern Legend"?

B. Listening

You are going to hear someone talk about James Dean. Before you listen, study these questions. Then answer them after you have listened to the cassette.

1. How did the speaker first happen to hear about James Dean?
2. What did the speaker and his friend do together one evening?
3. How did the speaker's friend feel when he saw Dean in the movie?
4. Why did the speaker's friend feel this way?
5. What does the speaker say was so strange or peculiar about Dean?

"Die young, and make a beautiful corpse," he used to say to his friends. And that was exactly what he did.

James Dean was not very tall—he was less than average height. He had thick, light brown hair and intense blue eyes. He was so near-sighted that he could hardly see anything without his glasses.

He came to Hollywood when he was eighteen, hoping to get into the movies. At first, he was not successful at all, and for a time he was so short of money that he had to live entirely on dry oatmeal, which he sometimes mixed with marmalade. Then he went to New York, the center of live theater in the United States. He got a part in a play and was seen by the great director Elia Kazan. Kazan was planning the movie *East of Eden* and realized Dean would be perfect for one of the main roles.

By this time, Dean already had a reputation for being eccentric and difficult to work with. He almost always wore the same overcoat and jeans, he rarely shaved, and he had hardly any friends at all. "If he didn't like you, he wouldn't even give you the pleasure of his anger. You could be in the same telephone booth with him, but you wouldn't exist," someone who knew him said later. When he went to parties, he often brought his bongo drums with him. Then he would sit in a corner, take off his glasses so that he couldn't see anybody, and play the drums all night without saying a word.

He went back to Hollywood to make *East of Eden* and then made two more movies, *Rebel Without a Cause* and *Giant*. His co-star in the last movie, Rock Hudson, later said "I didn't like Dean particularly. He was hard to be around. He was always angry and full of contempt. He never smiled."

In spite of his poor eyesight, he loved driving fast motorcycles and even faster sports cars. A few days after he finished *Giant*, on September 25, 1955, Dean went for a drive in his new Porsche. It was evening. The sun was going down and the light was poor. Dean was not wearing his glasses. Suddenly, he saw a car in front of him. It was slowing down and trying to turn off the highway. Dean tried to slow down too, but it was too late. He hit the car at high speed and was killed immediately.

Two German girls killed themselves when they heard the news because "life would be unbearable without him." A few years later, a New York salesclerk wrote a book called *Jimmy Dean Returns* in which she claimed that she was in contact with Dean from the other side of the grave. Half a million copies of the book were sold. It was only the beginning of a strange legend that goes on, even today.

▶ C. Reading

Read the article about James Dean. Then do the exercises that follow the article.

1. Find the words in the article that mean:

1. a dead body
2. strange in behavior
3. someone who opposes or fights people in power
4. the feeling that someone or something deserves no respect
5. so bad it is impossible to live with or tolerate
6. a place where a dead person is buried

2. Give your opinion. Do your classmates agree?

1. Why do you think Dean was regarded as "eccentric"?
2. Imagine you met Dean at a party in New York in the 1950s. What do you think you would say about him afterwards?
3. What exactly do you think Rock Hudson meant when he said "He was hard to be around"?
4. Whose fault do you think the accident on September 25, 1955 was? Give your reasons.
5. Describe some of the events that helped build a legend after his death.
6. When George Stevens, the director of *Giant*, heard of Dean's death, he said, "The way he drove, he had it coming to him." What do you think he meant?

3. Can you think of any other people who could be called "modern legends"? If so, what do you know about one of these people?

▶ D. Pronunciation: Words and Sounds

Listen to these sentences. Pay attention to the meaning of the words *live* and *lead*. Why does the pronunciation change?

1. When did Dean **live**?
2. New York is the center of **live** theater in the United States.
3. Movie stars often **lead** exciting lives.
4. This gas contains **lead**.

Can you think of any other words that are spelled the same but have different pronunciations? For example:

5. Do you **read** often?
6. I **read** an interesting novel last week.
7. It's raining and I forgot to **close** my car windows.
8. Did you park **close** to school?

2 LANGUAGE STUDY

A. The Past Progressive and the Simple Past

1. What's the difference between these two sentences?

1. What was Dean doing when he saw the car in front of him?
2. What did Dean do when he saw the car in front of him?

Which question gets the answer "He was driving very fast in his new Porsche"? What is the answer to the other question?

Now imagine that you have an alarm clock and that it went off at 6:00 this morning. How would you answer these two questions?

3. What were you doing when the alarm clock went off this morning?
4. What did you do when the alarm clock went off this morning?

2. Complete these sentences with the Past Progressive (*was/wasn't/were/weren't . . . ing*).

1. He (*drive*) on the highway when he had an accident.
2. He (*not watch*) the road, so he didn't see the car in front of him.
3. The people in the car in front (*drive*) slowly.
4. They (*listen*) to the radio as they drove.
5. They (*talk*) about marriage when their car was hit.
6. Luckily, they (*not go*) too fast and they (*wear*) their seat belts.

3. Look at these sentences. Have these things ever happened to you? If so, describe what you were doing when they happened.

Example   You realized you didn't have your car keys.
I was just leaving the house when I realized I didn't have my car keys.

1. A car almost hit you.
2. You suddenly began to feel sick.
3. Something made you laugh.
4. A stranger asked you for directions.

4. Have these things ever happened to you? If so, explain what you did.

Example   A stranger asked you for directions.
I stopped and told the stranger how to get there.

1. It started to rain and you were outside.
2. You came across a word you didn't understand.
3. You were in a restaurant when you began to feel very sick.
4. You heard a strange noise in the middle of the night.

5. Complete these sentences with the Simple Past or the Past Progressive.

1. My wife and I (*walk*) down the street when we ran into my old girlfriend.
2. When I noticed her, she (*stand*) in front of the movie theater with her arm around a very handsome man.
3. She and the man (*laugh*) about something when they turned and she saw me.
4. She (*whisper*) something into the man's ear, and then he looked at me too.
5. I (*not know*) what to do when she said hello.
6. I still liked her, but I (*not want*) to talk to her.
7. We (*chat*) politely when I realized who the man was.
8. It was Gregory Taylor and he (*star*) in the movie we were about to see.

Two of the verbs in the sentences above—*see* and *like*—are not usually used in the progressive form. There are two others. Do you know which ones they are?

6. On a personal level. Choose a time and talk with your partner about what you were both doing the past two nights.

	You	Your Partner
What were you doing at exactly 9 o'clock last night?		
Were you . . . at 9 o'clock the night before too?		

Now tell the class about yourself and your partner. Make sentences like the ones in the examples.

Examples *At 9 o'clock last night, Tony was watching TV. While he was watching TV, I was writing a letter.*

At the same time the night before, Tony was doing his homework. I was too.

B. Vocabulary Development

1. How do these verbs change when they become nouns? Complete these sentences with the noun form of the verb in parentheses.

Example (*live*) What do you know about his ....?
What do you know about his life?

1. (*see*) James Dean had very poor eye............
2. (*die*) His .... was reported in all the newspapers.
3. (*please*) It was not always a great .... meeting him.
4. (*compete*) He didn't know if he'd get the main role in the movie. There was a lot of ....
5. (*succeed*) Everyone wished him a lot of ....
6. (*mix*) He ate a .... of oatmeal and marmalade.
7. (*excite*) His movies caused a great deal of ....

Now use this chart to check your answers.

Verb	Noun	Verb	Noun
live	life	exist	existence
die	death	perform	performance
see	sight	refuse	refusal
pass	passage	excite	excitement
succeed	success	please	pleasure
mix	mixture	compete	competition

2. Look in the chart above for the words in *italics* in the sentences below. Then complete the sentences with the corresponding verb or noun form.

1. Yesterday I was fortunate to *see* two of the main .... here in Los Angeles—Disneyland and Hollywood.
2. That was quite a *performance*! In fact, I don't think I've ever seen anybody .... so well before.
3. I thought he would help me, but he *refused*. Actually, his .... surprised me.
4. Life .... very fast, but we often don't notice this quick *passage* of time until we are older.
5. I can *exist* on my salary. I mean, I have enough to eat and a place to sleep. But it's a boring ....
6. Thousands of athletes .... in the Olympic Games, and the *competition* among them is very intense.

C. Pronunciation

1. 📼 Stress and Intonation. Listen to the conversations, paying attention to the stress and intonation of the words in *italics*. Then practice the conversations.

1. A: Have you seen "Giant"?
   B: No, I haven't. *Have you?*
   A: No.

2. A: Did you like it?
   B: Yes. *Did you?*
   A: Not really.

3. A: Are you bored?
   B: No. *Are you?*
   A: Yes, a little.

4. A: I've seen that movie.
   B: Oh, *have you?*
   A: Yes.

5. A: I really liked it.
   B: Oh, *did you?* Why?
   A: I like everything James Dean did.

6. A: I'm bored.
   B: Oh, *are you?* Why?
   A: I don't have anything to do.

Complete B's part and read these conversations aloud. Then listen to them and check your pronunciation.

7. A: Do you understand this?
   B: No. .... you?
   A: I think so.

8. A: It's clear to me now.
   B: Oh, ... it? Good!
   A: Yes. Thanks for your help.

2. 📼 Words and Sounds. Listen to these groups of words. The vowel sound—the sound of the letters in bold—in one word in each group is different. Which one is it?

1. n**igh**t   s**igh**t   h**eigh**t   w**eigh**t
2. **Ea**st   D**ea**n   j**ea**ns   pl**ea**sure
3. **i**deal   r**ea**l   r**ea**lize   r**ea**lity
4. d**oo**r   m**o**re   c**o**rpse   c**o**lor
5. mi**ll**ion   bi**ll**ion   mi**ll**ionaire   **l**ion

Now say the words aloud.

▶ UNIT 3

3 DESCRIPTION

A. Describing People

Imagine you were in a restaurant in Los Angeles or New York a few days ago and saw these people there. You want to describe them now to a friend. Think of at least one thing you could say about each of them.

B. Matching

Study the comments below. Can you guess who each comment is about?

a. I'd say she was in her late 30s or early 40s. She was very beautiful with blond hair.
b. He was middle-aged.
c. I'm sure her hair was dyed, or maybe she was wearing a wig.
d. He was an ordinary-looking man. I'd say he was in his 40s.
e. She was wearing a plain dress, in a pale color. I had the impression she was from South America or somewhere like that.
f. His hair was thin and looked greasy, and it was parted in the middle. And he was wearing sunglasses.
g. She looked very strange. It was all that heavy makeup, especially around her eyes and mouth . . . and the color of her hair!
h. He was dressed very formally and looked like a successful politician or businessman.
i. She was in her late teens, with big, dark eyes.
j. She was dressed simply but elegantly, and was wearing a beautiful pearl necklace.
k. He had a beard and looked like a man who eats well.
l. She was the most unusual person I've ever seen. I mean, her hair was spiked and she was dressed in black leather.

Look at the pictures and comments again. Is there anyone above you think hasn't been described? If so, how would you describe him or her?

4 LANGUAGE STUDY

A. Vocabulary Development

1. Look at the diagram below. When we describe people, we usually concentrate on certain physical characteristics (1–5) and on certain aspects of the person's personality (6).

1 general appearance
2 hair
3 face, eyes, etc.
4 clothes
5 body size and "image"
6 attitude toward other people

Now study the list below. Which of the characteristics or qualities above (1–6) do you think each word or phrase refers to?

- aggressive
- attractive
- average height
- bald
- casually dressed
- conceited
- curly
- dark
- dirty
- dyed
- elegant
- friendly
- handsome
- long
- overweight
- pretty
- reserved
- rude
- serious
- shy
- sloppy
- tall
- thin
- well-dressed

2. Study the chart below. Use it to check your answers in Exercise 1.

Physical Characteristics and Personal Qualities			
Body	**Hair**	**General Appearance**	**Personality**
average height	black	attractive	aggressive
short/tall	blond	beautiful/pretty	conceited
average weight	brown	good-looking/	easygoing
thin/fat	red	handsome	friendly
overweight	gray	casually/	funny
	white	well-dressed	generous
Eyes		dirty	kind
black	dark/light	elegant	outgoing
blue	curly/straight	light/dark	reserved
brown	short/long	sloppy	rude
gray	dyed	young/old	serious
green		middle-aged	shy
hazel	bald		snobbish
dark		have a beard/	
		mustache	
		wear glasses	

Do you know any other words or phrases that you can use to describe people?

3. Choose the appropriate words in parentheses to complete this description of the person in the diagram in Exercise 1.

He isn't really very (¹ *good-looking/beautiful*). He has (² *light/dark*) hair and a (³ *light/dark*) complexion. He is (⁴ *casually dressed/well-dressed*) in jeans, a sports coat, and a tie. His eyes are (⁵ *blue/hazel*)—they're not really blue and they're not really green, and they seem to have a little brown in them. As far as his personality, he's not very (⁶ *outgoing/reserved*). In fact, he's pretty shy. But he's a very (⁷ *kind/rude*) person and he loves animals.

4. On a Personal Level

1. Describe yourself to your classmates. Answer these two questions:
   a. What do you look like?
   b. What are you like?
2. Describe a classmate or a famous person (a movie star, a rock star, a politician, etc.). See if your classmates can guess who you are describing.
3. What personal qualities do you think the ideal man or woman should have?

B. Idioms That Use Parts of the Body

1. Choose the correct meaning of these expressions.

1. His heart is in the right place.
   a. He doesn't need an operation.
   b. He is very kind.
   c. He is perfectly normal.
2. It turned my stomach!
   a. I felt disgusted.
   b. I really enjoyed it.
   c. I got very hungry.
3. I didn't ask her for a date because I got cold feet.
   a. ... because my feet began to feel cold.
   b. ... because I lost my courage.
   c. ... because I didn't know her phone number.
4. You've got baseball on the brain.
   a. Your head looks like a baseball.
   b. You think only about baseball.
   c. You are crazy!
5. Keep your fingers crossed.
   a. Hope for the best.
   b. Shake hands and agree.
   c. Don't do anything.
6. All this is over my head.
   a. I can't understand it.
   b. It isn't my fault!
   c. I can't afford it.
7. Go on. Get it off your chest!
   a. Wash your chest.
   b. Say what you want to say.
   c. Take your shirt off.
8. I'm up to my ears in work.
   a. I don't like my job.
   b. I use my ears a lot in my job.
   c. I have too much to do.

2. On a personal level. Tell your classmates about:

1. someone you think has his or her heart in the right place. Say why you think so.
2. something that turns your stomach.
3. a time when you got cold feet.
4. something your best friend has on the brain.
5. a time when you might keep your fingers crossed.
6. a subject that is over your head.
7. a time when you had to get something off your chest.
8. someone who is up to his or her ears in personal problems.

3. Try to figure out what these expressions mean.

1. *Keep an eye on* this for me, will you?
2. You *have a good ear for* languages.
3. I'm really *sticking my neck out* for you.
4. He said some terrible things about me *behind my back*! It seems he's *always talking behind someone's back*!
5. Don't *lose your head*.
6. This story will *break your heart*.
7. I didn't *have the heart to* tell him the bad news.
8. *Keep your nose out of* this.
9. *Keep your chin up*.
10. *You're pulling my leg*!

Which of the sentences above means:

a. Stop interfering.
b. I'm taking a big risk.
c. Be calm!

What do the others mean?

4. Complete the sentences with an expression from Exercise 3. Use the tense suggested in parentheses.

Example She played the piano and the guitar. She .... music. (Simple Past)
She played the piano and the guitar. She had a good ear for music.

1. My brother .... my house if I go to New York. (Future)
2. I didn't believe a word he said. He .... (Past Progressive)
3. Everyone in the movie theater was crying. The story was so sad, it .... (Simple Past)
4. I didn't ask for your opinion. Please .... my business. (Imperative)
5. My daughter's cat is sick and I .... tell her. (Simple Present)
6. You want to marry him? Really? I mean, he's very handsome and outgoing. But .... He doesn't have a job and he doesn't have any money. (Negative Imperative)
7. I thought she liked me, but she's been saying things that aren't true about me. I don't like it when someone .... like that. (Simple Present)
8. .... It isn't as bad as you think, and I'm sure everything will be all right. (Imperative)

5 READING, LISTENING, AND WRITING

A. Reading

After you read the article, say what you think was unusual about the person. What did he look like?

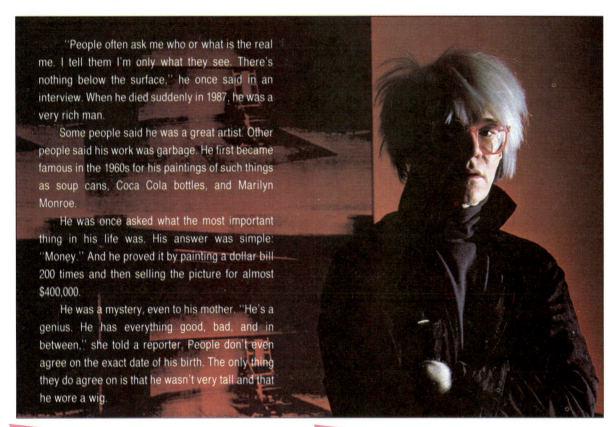

"People often ask me who or what is the real me. I tell them I'm only what they see. There's nothing below the surface," he once said in an interview. When he died suddenly in 1987, he was a very rich man.

Some people said he was a great artist. Other people said his work was garbage. He first became famous in the 1960s for his paintings of such things as soup cans, Coca Cola bottles, and Marilyn Monroe.

He was once asked what the most important thing in his life was. His answer was simple: "Money." And he proved it by painting a dollar bill 200 times and then selling the picture for almost $400,000.

He was a mystery, even to his mother. "He's a genius. He has everything good, bad, and in between," she told a reporter. People don't even agree on the exact date of his birth. The only thing they do agree on is that he wasn't very tall and that he wore a wig.

B. Listening

The day after he died, they talked about the person above on a radio program. Listen to the program and then answer the questions.

1. What was the man's name?
2. Where and when was he born?
3. How or why did he become famous?
4. What kind of impression did he make on other people?
5. In what way was his own life-style different from that of many of the people around him?
6. What else besides his painting was he famous for?

C. Speaking

Prepare a short talk about a famous person. When you give the talk, don't mention the person's name. See if your audience can guess who you are talking about. Here are some phrases that may help you:

He/She was born in . . . around the year . . .
He/She is a . . ./works for . . .
This person was famous for . . ./as a . . .
Some people say that he/she was . . . (one opinion of the person's work)
Other people say . . . (another opinion of that person's work)

D. Writing

Write a short article about the person you talked about in Exercise C. Be sure to mention the same facts that you mentioned in the talk. However, in the article, also give the person's name.

UNIT 4 A Different World

1 DISCUSSION AND READING

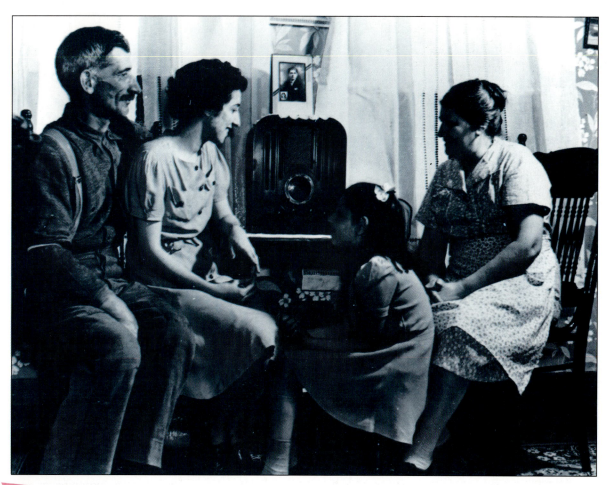

A. Discussion

Look at the photograph and discuss these questions.

1. When do you think the photograph was taken? Explain why you think so.
   a. More than a hundred years ago
   b. Forty or maybe even fifty years ago
   c. Only a few years ago

2. How well-off do you think these people are or were? Explain why you think so.
   a. They are very poor.
   b. They are very rich.
   c. They are not poor, but they are not very well-off either.

3. Imagine you could walk into the other rooms of the house where this photograph was taken. Try to describe these other rooms. Would they be large or small? What are some of the things you might find in the rooms?

4. If this were a photograph of a living room today, what are some of the things you might find there? What do you think the people would be doing?

B. Reading

Read this account of someone's childhood. Then do the exercises.

I was born and grew up in a small town in northern California. I lived with my parents, my grandmother, and my two younger brothers. We weren't well-off, but we didn't think of ourselves as poor. My father was a mechanic and he always had a lot of work.

When I was five, I started school. It was an old, run-down building and we sat on hard wooden seats. Some of the other boys and girls used to get very bored, but for me school was a great adventure. The only teacher I didn't like very much was Mr. Parr, who had very bad breath and sometimes used to drink too much at lunchtime and fall asleep in the middle of the afternoon.

At home we never used to talk very much at mealtimes. After dinner my father used to go back to the garage and repair cars. As soon as they were old enough, my two brothers started helping him. I used to do my homework in the kitchen every evening while my mother and grandmother washed the dishes and cleaned up the kitchen. On Saturday nights, we would all sit in the living room and listen to the radio. That was our only entertainment in those days. The rest of the time I read. I liked reading even then, but I had very few books.

When I was fourteen, I started high school. My teachers said I was very bright, and later I got a scholarship to the University of California in Los Angeles. My father didn't like the idea very much, but my mother told him "a girl with a college education can find a better husband." I remember that once my father told me not to read so many books because "people who read too much go blind." He was serious.

The real problem came after I graduated and I told him I wanted to continue studying. He couldn't understand why I didn't get married and have children.

Sometimes I go back to the town where I was born. My parents died a few years ago, but my brothers are still there. One of them sells used cars and the other owns a gas station. It isn't easy to talk to them anymore. Perhaps it never was. We never really knew each other very well. There is something like an invisible wall between us. I am on one side, and they are on the other.

1. Answer *True* or *False*. Give reasons for each answer.

1. The writer came from a family with a lot of money.
2. The writer's father worked hard.
3. The first school the writer went to was not very comfortable.
4. Mr. Parr was probably a popular teacher.
5. The evenings the writer describes are just like the evenings you spend at home.
6. At mealtimes, the writer and her brothers learned a lot from their parents about life and about the world.
7. The writer's father thought education was a good thing.
8. The writer feels different from her brothers now.

2. One of these people wrote the text. Which one? Give reasons for your answer.

1. Irene Charlton, now fifty-five, professor of psychology at New York University.
2. Cheryl Laughton, a nurse in the town of Barston, California.
3. Jack Allford, forty-nine, ex-mechanic, now working in a factory in northern California.

2 LANGUAGE STUDY

A. The Past with *used to*

1. Study these sentences.

1. I live in California.
2. I used to live in California.
3. I smoke forty cigarettes a day.
4. I used to smoke forty cigarettes a day.
5. I usually get up at five and go to bed at midnight.
6. I used to get up at five and go to bed at midnight.

Now find the appropriate response to each of the sentences above.

a. Don't you get tired by the end of the day?
b. Did you? In what part?
c. That was a lot, wasn't it?
d. Didn't you get very tired by the end of the day?
e. Do you? In what part?
f. That's a lot, isn't it?

Which words in the responses (a–f) make them the right responses to sentences 1–6?

2. Complete these statements with *used to* or *didn't use to* and the verb in parentheses.

Examples   When I was little, I (*live*) on a farm.
When I was little, I used to live on a farm.

I (*not live*) in the city like I do now.
I didn't use to live in the city like I do now.

1. Life (*be*) different in those days.
2. I remember our nearest neighbors (*live*) five miles away from us.
3. But I (*not feel*) lonely.
4. I had two brothers and two sisters and we (*play*) together.
5. We didn't have a television like other people, but we never (*think*) about it.
6. We (*like*) helping our parents and feeding the animals.
7. Mom and Dad (*get up*) at 5 o'clock every day and begin working.
8. In fact, we all (*be*) busy from early morning until late at night.

3. 🔊 Listen to the pronunciation of the words and sounds. Then say the sentences aloud. When does the sound *s* change?

1. I use my car a lot.
2. I used my car yesterday.
3. I used to walk everywhere.
4. I never used to drive anywhere.
5. I can't get used to driving in the city.

Can you explain the meaning of each sentence? Choose one of the explanations below.

a. I drove my car yesterday.
b. I can't get accustomed to driving in the city.
c. I drive my car a lot.
d. I never drove anywhere before because I didn't have a car.
e. I walked everywhere before I got my car.

4. These statements are all untrue. Disagree with them by using *used to* or *never used to*.

Example   People have always traveled by plane.
That's not true. People never used to travel by plane.

1. Women have always gone to college.
2. Men have always taken care of the children, cooked, and cleaned.
3. The United States never produced more cars than Japan.
4. The average person has always owned a car.
5. Most people in Europe and America never died before they were forty.
6. The air in most cities has never been clean.
7. Pollution has always been a big problem.
8. Mexico City, New York, and Tokyo were never small cities.
9. Movies have always been more popular than TV.
10. People have always had a lot of money to spend on leisure-time activities.

5. On a personal level. Complete these questions.

Example .... you ever (*get*) lonely when you were little?
Did you ever use to get lonely when you were little?

1. Where .... you (*live*) when you were little?
2. .... your mother and father (*spend*) a lot of time with you?
3. What .... you (*do*) after school?
4. .... you (*have*) a lot of friends to play with?
5. What kind of games or sports .... you (*play*)?
6. .... you (*have*) any pets—like a dog or a cat?
7. What .... you (*like*) most about being a child?

Now interview a classmate. Use the questions above and find out about your classmate's childhood. Take notes so you can then tell the class about the person you interviewed.

B. Reflexive and Reciprocal Pronouns

1. What's the difference between these two sentences?

1. My father and my brothers always helped each other.
2. My father and my brothers always helped themselves.

Which sentence means "My father and my brothers did things without help from other people"? What does the other sentence mean?

2. Complete the sentences with *yourself, themselves, ourselves,* or *each other*.

1. Sit down! Make .... at home!
2. All the people at the party are helping .... to the food on the table.
3. Bill, Laura, and I have known .... for years.
4. All the students got into pairs and asked .... questions about their hobbies.
5. That young man and young woman have been looking at .... across the room.
6. The people here are very friendly. They all know .... very well.
7. No one else will help us, so we'll have to help ....
8. You can see that those two love .... very much.

C. *Only a little* and *only a few*

Can you figure out when to use *only a little* or *only a few* in these sentences? Pay special attention to the words that *only a little* or *only a few* refer to.

1. In the past, ... people had the opportunity to get a good education.
2. I've met .... men who really understand the difficulties women have in business.
3. There's .... gas left in the tank.
4. A: How much milk do you want in your coffee?
   B: ...., please.
5. Someone once said that .... knowledge of a subject was more dangerous than none at all.
6. I speak .... words of Japanese.
7. I speak .... Japanese.
8. .... of the students in the class really understood what the teacher was saying.

D. On a Personal Level

Discuss these questions.

1. Think of things that people in your country never used to do, but which they do now—or things which they used to do, but don't do now.
2. Have people in your country always had the opportunity to get a good education? Give reasons for your answer.
3. What does this English expression mean: *God helps those who help themselves*. Is there a similar expression in your language? Do you think it's true?

3 READING AND DISCUSSION

A. Reading

1. This is part of an article that appeared in a newspaper recently. It is in seven parts. However, only the first part (A) is in the right place. Can you put the other parts in the right order?

Changes in the Way We Live

A More people in the United States have washing machines, televisions, and cars today than they did in 1946. They also have more fear of violence and crime. Whereas once the nation's heroes used to be

B changed considerably. People dress much more casually than they used to. And whereas "an evening out" for most people used to mean a trip to the movie theater, today it is much more likely to involve going to a restaurant or to a disco. Some things have not changed. People still adore the films of Humphrey Bogart and Ingrid Bergman even though they are more likely to watch them on television or on videocassette. And in spite of

C like beer or wine with their meal instead of coffee. In 1946 only a small proportion—less than 10 percent—ever drank alcohol with their meals. One of the most surprising things to come out of this new research is the lack of ambition among the middle-aged. Many men and women—including some business executives—feel that by the

D survey made in 1946. In many cases, the new survey tells us what we already knew, such as the fact that many people are better off in a material sense and that women spend much less time at the kitchen sink or in the home taking care of their families. However, we also learn a number of other things. For example, tastes in clothing and entertainment have

E time they are in their late forties or early fifties, they have worked enough. Most of them said they would prefer to retire than go on working for more money or a promotion.

F soldiers or politicians, today they are more likely to be famous faces from television or the movies, such as Sylvester Stallone. These are just some of the changes discovered in a survey by the Market Research Association. More than 3,000 people were questioned, and the results were compared with a similar

G the variety of foreign food now available, more than a quarter of the people in the survey said they still preferred a meal of steak and potatoes. The only change is that a large number would also

2. Find the words in the text that mean:

1. use of force to hurt or harm
2. people you admire for their bravery or other qualities
3. a series of questions about particular themes or topics which many different people answer
4. part, percentage
5. desire for success, power, "getting ahead in life"
6. people in business who make important decisions
7. to stop working when you get to a certain age; usually sixty or sixty-five
8. a better job in the same company

B. Discussion

Find out from other people in your class what they think some of the most important changes in their country have been with regard to such things as:

1. entertainment
2. clothing
3. food
4. work

Are there other aspects of life in your country that have changed?

4 LANGUAGE STUDY

A. Using *like* and *prefer*

1. Study the beginnings of these sentences. Can you match the beginning of each one with its appropriate ending (a–d)? Each sentence can be ended in only one way.

1. I like the movies . . .
2. I like going to the movies . . .
3. I prefer the movies . . .
4. I prefer going to the movies . . .

a. to watching television.
b. more than watching television.
c. to television.
d. more than television.

2. Complete these sentences with *like* or *prefer*.

1. When I was younger, I used to .... watching cartoons and baseball games at home more than going to a movie at a theater.
2. Now I'm older and .... seeing a new movie or reading a good book to sitting in front of the TV.
3. I mean, I .... seeing or reading something serious to dealing with the junk they show on TV these days.
4. And when I do watch TV, I .... humorous programs or programs about animals and nature more than programs about crime and violence.
5. See, I'm a cop and I .... my job more than anything else, but I get enough crime and violence at work. When I'm home, I want to relax and have fun.

3. Interview a classmate using this questionnaire. Write down the answers, using numbers and letters, for example, 1a, 2b, etc. If any of the answers below are not appropriate, your classmate should give an answer in his or her own words.

1. In general, which of these two things would you say you usually prefer doing?
   a. watching television
   b. listening to the radio

2. If you had a choice, what would you prefer to do the next time you go on vacation?
   a. go abroad
   b. stay in your own country

3. Imagine that you want to invite someone for dinner this evening, and that time and money are really no problem. What would you prefer to do?
   a. take your friend to a nice restaurant
   b. buy what you need and cook a good meal at home

4. When you go to a party where there are people your own age who you don't know, which of these two things are you more likely to do?
   a. dress casually (jeans, tennis shoes, etc.)
   b. dress more formally (shirt and tie for men, dresses for women)

5. What do you think you'll probably do if you have the choice?
   a. retire with a good pension before the age of 55
   b. continue working for as long as possible

6. What's your favorite way of having a good time at the end of the week?
   a. going to a disco
   b. staying at home and watching TV
   c. seeing friends or having parties

7. Which of these goals do you regard as the most important to you at the moment?
   a. improving your education
   b. getting a promotion at work
   c. buying a car

8. What do you think is more important in life?
   a. material success
   b. relationships with your family and friends
   c. a lot of leisure time

▶ UNIT 4

4. With the answers to the questionnaire in front of you, tell someone else or the class what you found out about the person you interviewed. For example, for question 1, you could say something like this:

"In general, she/he prefers listening to the radio to watching television. But a lot depends on the program."

5. On a personal level. Write a few sentences summing up your own answers to the questions. For example, for question 1, you could write an answer like this:

"In general, I prefer watching television to listening to the radio but sometimes I enjoy listening to the radio too. For example, when I'm studying, it's nice to listen to some quiet music."

B. Comparing Things with *more/less/fewer . . . than*

1. Study these sentences.

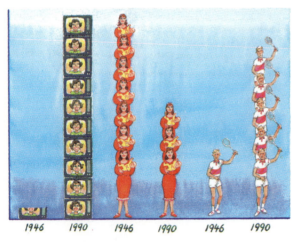

1. Today, more people have televisions than they did in 1946.
2. In 1946, fewer people had televisions than they do now.
3. Women spend much less time in the home now than they did in the 1940s.
4. Today, people have more free time than they've ever had before.

Can you explain when you have to use *less* and when you have to use *fewer*?

2. Complete these sentences with *more (than)*, *less (than)*, or *fewer (than)*.

1. In 1946, the world's economy was growing so there was .... unemployment in the United States and Europe .... there is today.
2. There weren't as many robberies and murders, so there was also .... fear of crime.
3. In those days, ... men and women were likely to go to a restaurant or to a night club. They couldn't afford those things.
4. In 1946, ... people preferred coffee or tea with their meals .... wine. Wine wasn't common and it was expensive.
5. And you could find .... foreign food in the stores and restaurants .... you can now. Today we eat all kinds of food from other countries.
6. In general, people live better today. But there are still .... families in the world that are well-off .... are poor.

C. Pronunciation: Words and Sounds

1. 📼 Listen to these sentences. Pay special attention to the words in bold. Then read the sentences aloud.

1. I need some **cloth**.
2. I bought two **tablecloths**.
3. Tastes in **clothing** have changed.
4. Where do you buy your **clothes**?

2. Say these words. Which ones have the same vowel sound as *cloth*? Which ones have the same vowel sound as *clothes*?

1. go	4. soft	7. office	10. cold
2. roast	5. off	8. told	11. offer
3. know	6. cost	9. close	12. coffee

33

5 LISTENING AND WRITING

A. Listening

Listen to these four people talk about changes in their lives. Then do the exercises below.

George Black

Mike Lopez

Carol Simpson

Cheryl Laughton

1. 📼 Listen to the two men, George and Mike, first. Then decide if these statements are true or false.

1. One man's life has changed a lot, but the other's hasn't changed at all.
2. Neither of the men seems to worry about money very much.
3. One of the men seems to worry more about his health than the other one does.

2. Describe to a classmate an important change in one of the men's lives. See if your classmate can describe any changes in the other man's life.

3. 📼 Now listen to the two women, Carol and Cheryl. Then discuss answers to these questions.

1. Do you think Carol prefers her life today to her life three years ago? Give reasons for your answer.
2. Try to imagine a typical day in Cheryl's life.
3. What do you think Cheryl means when she says, "We can do the things *we* want to do now."
4. There is one change in both women's lives that is similar. What is it?

B. Writing

1. First talk about yourself.

1. Think back to a time when your life was different. Briefly tell about a typical day in your life at that time.
2. Now compare it with a typical day in your life now. Talk about what is different. Is anything the same? Is anything better or worse than it used to be?

2. In about 200 words, write down what you have said above.

LANGUAGE SUMMARY FOR UNIT 3

1. Saying what you were doing and what you did when . . .

What was Dean doing when he saw the car in front of him?
  He was driving very fast in his new Porsche.
What did Dean do when he saw the car in front of him?
  He tried to slow down, but it was too late.
I was just leaving the house when I realized I didn't have my car keys.
  When a stranger asked me for directions, I stopped and told her how to get there.

2. Saying what you were doing while . . .

At 9 o'clock last night, Tony was watching TV.
While he was watching TV, I was writing a letter.

3. Vocabulary Development: Verb and Noun Forms

Verb	Noun	Verb	Noun
live	life	exist	existence
die	death	perform	performance
see	sight	refuse	refusal
pass	passage	excite	excitement
succeed	success	please	pleasure
mix	mixture	compete	competition

I thought he would help me, but he refused. His refusal surprised me.

4. Vocabulary Development: Physical Characteristics and Personal Qualities

Body
average height
short/tall
average weight
thin/fat
overweight

Eyes
black
blue
brown
gray
green
hazel
dark

Hair
black
blond
brown
red
gray
white

dark/light
curly/straight
short/long
bald
dyed

General Appearance
attractive
beautiful/pretty
good-looking/handsome
casually dressed/
well-dressed
dirty
elegant
light/dark
sloppy
young/old
middle-aged

have a beard/mustache
wear glasses

Personality
aggressive
conceited
easygoing
friendly
funny
generous
kind
outgoing
reserved
rude
serious
shy
snobbish

He has light hair and a light complexion.
I think his eyes are hazel.
He's not very outgoing, but he's a very kind person.

5. Idioms that use parts of the body

His heart is in the right place.
It turned my stomach!
I didn't ask her for a date because I got cold feet.
You've got baseball on the brain.
Keep your fingers crossed.
All this is over my head.
Get it off your chest!
I'm up to my ears in work.
Keep an eye on this for me, will you?
You have a good ear for languages.
I'm really sticking my neck out for you.
He said some terrible things about me behind my back!
Don't lose your head.
This story will break your heart.
I didn't have the heart to tell him the bad news.
Keep your nose out of this.
Keep your chin up.
You're pulling my leg.

6. Pronunciation

Stress and Intonation:

I've seen that movie.
  Oh, have you?
Yes.

Do you understand this?
  No. Do you?
I think so.

Words and Sounds:

Where did Dean **live**?
New York is the center of **live** theater in the U.S.
Movie stars **lead** exciting lives.
This gas contains **lead**.

n**igh**t s**igh**t h**eigh**t w**eigh**t
East **D**ean j**ea**ns pl**ea**sure
id**ea**l r**ea**l r**ea**lize r**ea**lity
d**oo**r m**o**re c**o**rpse c**o**lor
mill**ion** bill**ion** milli**o**naire li**on**

LANGUAGE SUMMARY FOR UNIT 4

1. Talking about the past with *used to*

A: When I was little, I used to live on a farm. I didn't use to live in the city like I do now.
B: Did you ever use to get lonely?
A: Yes. I didn't use to have a lot of friends to play with. And my parents never used to spend a lot of time with me.

2. Using reflexive and reciprocal pronouns

Sit down! Make yourself at home!
All the people at the party are helping themselves to the food on the table.

Bill, Laura, and I have known each other for years.
You can see that those two love each other very much.

3. Talking about how many or how much with *only a little* and *only a few*

In the past, only a few people had the opportunity to get a good education.
Someone once said that only a little knowledge of a subject was more dangerous than none at all.
I speak only a few words of Japanese.
I speak only a little Japanese.

4. Making comparisons with *more/less/fewer...than*

Today, more people have televisions than they did in 1946.
In 1946, fewer people had cars than they do now.
Women spend much less time in the home now than they did in the 1940s.
Today, people have more free time than they've ever had before.

5. Talking about preferences

I like humorous programs more than programs about crime.
I like going to the movies more than watching television.
I prefer wine to beer.
I prefer reading a book to watching television.

6. Pronunciation: Words and Sounds

I **use** my car a lot.
I **used** my car yesterday.
I **used** to walk everywhere.
I never **used** to drive anywhere.

I need some **cloth**.
I bought two table**cloths**.
Tastes in **clothing** have changed.
Where do you buy your **clothes**?

UNIT 5 Would You Eat It?

1 READING, LISTENING, AND DISCUSSION

A. Discussion

Look at the pictures and discuss these questions.

1. How many of the things here can you name?
2. How many of these things do you consider to be food?
3. Is there anything here which you would not eat but which is eaten in other countries? If so, what is it?
4. Why do you think certain things are eaten in some countries but not in others?
5. Describe a way of cooking two or three of these things.

B. Reading

Read these short descriptions of certain kinds of food. Ignore the words you don't understand and try to guess the names of the foods being described.

1. They are a basic part of the diet in many countries all over the world. They are round, grow in the ground, and have a thin skin, which is often peeled before they are cooked. They can be boiled, fried, or baked.
2. They are really a fruit, although many people regard them as a vegetable. They are soft, red, and round and were discovered in South America in the sixteenth century. They are often eaten raw in salads and are also cooked, especially when they are used in sauces for meat and other things.
3. They are a kind of flat shellfish and can be eaten either raw or cooked. They are now considered to be "food for the rich," although they were once so cheap that poor people ate them all the time.
4. This is one of the oldest vegetables in history. The ancient Greeks and Romans used to eat them raw for breakfast, with a little salt. They are round, with a thin skin which has to be removed before they can be cooked or eaten. They have a very strong smell and are often used to give flavor to soups, sauces, and other dishes.
5. This meat is very popular in some countries. However, in other countries people are forbidden to eat it because it is considered "impure."
6. These small animals live in sewers and other filthy places. They have very sharp teeth and will eat their way through almost anything. In one part of Belgium, a special type of this animal is cooked and eaten in a stew. According to people who have tried this dish, the meat tastes something like rabbit.
7. They are small, round, and full of juice. Some of them are dark or "red" and others are light or "green." They are used to make wine.
8. This is the seed of a plant which is grown in warm, wet places and eaten everywhere in the world, but particularly in China, Japan, and other Asian countries.
9. This insect causes famine when it comes in great numbers and eats all the crops. However, the ancient Egyptians used to enjoy eating it. It was usually roasted and then eaten whole, wings and all.
10. This is an eight-legged sea animal with a hard shell. The flesh can be eaten after boiling, when it turns bright red. It is closely related to insects, although people who pay high prices for it in restaurants do not often realize this.

Now answer these questions.

1. Name just one of the foods you were able to guess.
2. What were the words that helped you guess this food?
3. Now name the other foods you were able to guess. Give the words in the description which helped you guess each one.
4. Maybe you didn't know the names in English for some of the kinds of food that were described. Does this list contain any of those names?

- lobsters
- oysters
- leeks
- grapes
- broccoli
- chicken
- veal
- potatoes
- rats
- lettuce
- spiders
- ants
- apples
- rice
- pork
- oranges
- beef
- lamb
- flounder
- salmon
- tuna
- tomatoes
- peas
- carrots
- mice
- onions
- beans
- locusts

5. Which foods in the list above were not described?
6. Is there anything in the list that you do not consider food?

C. Listening

You are going to hear a short conversation between two people. Think about these questions as you listen.

1. What do you think they are talking about?
2. What are some of the words that helped you guess?

Now listen to the conversation again.

3. Did you learn anything new about this type of food? If so, what?

2 LANGUAGE STUDY

▼ A. The Passive Voice

1. Which two of these sentences mean more or less the same thing? Which two sentences have almost the same words but an important difference in meaning?

1. Poor people used to eat oysters.
2. Oysters used to be eaten by poor people.
3. They used to eat them for breakfast.
4. They used to be eaten for breakfast.

2. Make complete sentences. Match the part of the sentence on the left with the part on the right.

1. The Spaniards discovered
2. They were discovered
3. Sir Walter Raleigh
4. They were
5. They can be
6. You can
7. The French used to
8. They used to

a. took them to England fifty years later.
b. call them "love apples."
c. be called "love apples" in France.
d. cooked in many ways.
e. by the Spaniards in the 16th century in Peru.
f. cook them in many ways.
g. taken to England fifty years later.
h. them in Peru in the 16th century.

3. Complete these sentences with the correct passive form of the verb in parentheses (*is/are eaten*, *was/were discovered*, etc.).

Examples Potatoes (*discover*) in Peru in the 1500s.
Potatoes were discovered in Peru in the 1500s.

Today, they (*eat*) in many countries around the world.
Today, they are eaten in many countries around the world.

1. Do you know where the tomato (*discover*)?
2. Both the potato and the tomato (*discover*) in South America.
3. Tomatoes (*introduce*) to Europe in the 16th century.
4. Today, tomatoes (*grow*) worldwide.
5. More tomatoes (*produce*) by the United States, Italy, Brazil, Spain, and Japan than by any other countries.
6. Can you think of any other foods that (*find*) originally only in North or South America?
7. Can you think of any foods that (*not eat*) in your country in the 1500s?
8. What fruits and vegetables (*grow*) in your country?

4. Complete these sentences with the passive form.

Examples (*can/cook*) Potatoes .... many different ways.
Potatoes can be cooked many different ways.

(*used to/eat*) In some countries, they .... raw.
In some countries, they used to be eaten raw.

1. (*can/use*) Tomatoes .... in sauces and other dishes or eaten raw in salads.
2. (*used to/grow*) Rice .... mostly by people in South and East Asia.
3. (*can/find*) Today, rice crops .... in North America, South America, Europe, Africa, and Australia.
4. (*must/cook*) Rice .... before you can eat it.
5. (*should not/eat*) In some countries, people think that pork ....
6. (*have to/wash*) Potatoes grow in the ground and are often dirty. They .... before you can use them.
7. (*will/serve*) What time .... dinner ....?
8. (*should/serve*) According to the invitation, dinner .... promptly at 8:00.

5. Complete these sentences with the active (*consider/can consider/considered*) or passive (*are/can be/were considered*) form of the verb.

1. Today oysters (*consider*) "food for the rich."
2. However, a hundred years ago a lot of poor people (*eat*) them too.
3. Several years ago, large numbers of locusts (*destroy*) the crops in Africa.
4. Locusts (*used to eat*) by the ancient Egyptians.
5. Beer (*make*) in ancient Egypt.
6. Ordinary people in ancient Egypt (*often drink*) it for breakfast.
7. Today beer (*can find*) in almost every country.
8. However, it (*not usually drink*) for breakfast.

6. On a personal level. In pairs or in groups, talk about your country. Discuss these questions.

1. What kinds of fruits, vegetables, and grains are grown in your country?
2. What kinds of animals are raised for meat?
3. What kinds of fish are caught in the lakes, rivers, or ocean?
4. What foods or other products are imported by your country?
5. What foods or other products are exported?
6. Do you own anything that was made in another country, for example, a watch or a car? Where was it made?

B. Vocabulary Development

1. The words below all mean *cook*, but they are sometimes confused. Match the words with the pictures.

1. fry   3. boil   5. broil
2. bake   4. roast   6. grill

2. Use the word *cook* and the other words from Exercise 1 to complete these sentences. Change the form if necessary.

1. In the United States, a leg of lamb is usually .... in the oven.
2. Bread is .... in an oven.
3. If you are going to use onions in soup, you should .... them in a little oil first.
4. Americans are famous for their .... steaks.

5. What is one of the most common ways to cook vegetables? .... them in water.
6. French fries are long, thin slices of potato that are ....
7. Cakes, pies, cookies, and other pastries are usually .... in a hot oven.
8. If you think water isn't safe to drink, it should be .... first.
9. Some people .... their steaks or fish rather than fry it. They think it is less fattening.
10. Frying, baking, boiling, broiling, and roasting are methods of .... that are usually done on a stove inside. ...., sometimes called *barbecuing*, is usually done outside.

3. In pairs or in groups, discuss the answers to these questions. Then compare your answers with the answers of other pairs or groups.

1. What is something people always bake and never roast in the oven?
2. How many vegetables can you name that people usually eat raw rather than cooked?
3. Think of at least two different kinds of food other than meat that you can eat either fried or boiled.
4. What things do you enjoy eating grilled?

C. Pronunciation: Words and Sounds

1. 🔊 Listen to these groups of words. Pay special attention to the letters in bold. Which word does not belong in each group? Pronounce the words aloud.

1. p**ea**s   cr**ea**m   br**ea**d   b**ea**n
2. br**ea**d   p**e**pper   l**e**mon   l**ea**n
3. b**ea**n   b**ee**f   ch**ee**se   p**ea**r
4. b**ee**f   m**ea**l   p**i**zza   b**ee**n
5. f**i**sh   ch**i**cken r**i**pe   f**i**let
6. c**a**ke   st**ea**k   v**ea**l   b**a**ke

2. In the groups above, how many words can you find that have the same sound as *ea* in these words?

a. pea   b. steak   c. bread

3. Think of at least three more words (they don't have to be about food) that rhyme with *pear*.

3 READING AND THINKING

A. Reading

These four people were asked to talk about what they eat. Can you guess who is speaking? Give at least two reasons why you think so.

Maria Silva

Michio Ogawa

Carol Simpson

David Rider

1 "I eat a lot of foreign food: Italian, French, Mexican . . . that sort of thing. But I prefer something simpler—a piece of broiled fish or meat with a fresh vegetable and some rice. And of course, my favorite thing is sushi, raw fish. I think it's healthy for you. I like beer and wine a lot too, but it depends on what I'm eating."

2 "I'm just not very interested in food. I usually only have a cup of coffee and a bowl of cereal for breakfast, and I often skip lunch. For dinner, I might buy a can of soup or maybe a frozen dinner, and heat it up. Once in a while, I get something to take out from a Chinese restaurant or one of those fried chicken places. Oh . . . I eat a lot of chocolate. I guess I've got a sweet tooth. I never touch alcohol. It doesn't agree with me."

3 "Food is still one of life's mysteries to me. It's all my parents' fault. They're pretty conventional in their tastes. My mother insists on cooking things like pot roast or meatloaf, and she boils her vegetables to death. In fact, the kind of food I have to eat is so disgusting that I'd rather not talk about it, if you don't mind. I think I'd like to be a vegetarian, but it's awfully difficult to persuade my parents to change their habits!"

4 "I absolutely adore fish, particularly white fish, such as sole or haddock, cooked in a little white wine, with some garlic and lemon. And recently, I've been experimenting with Japanese food, particularly sashimi, raw fish. It's delicious, you know, if it's prepared right. Oh, and I love fresh vegetables such as carrots, broccoli, and asparagus, and fresh green beans. But I hate them overcooked. They're awful! Oh, and I'm extremely fond of pasta, but it has to be freshly made! It's absolutely delicious!"

B. Discussion

1. Give your opinion. Do your classmates agree?

1. Imagine a meal that each one of these people had yesterday. Describe it.
2. Which person would you prefer to eat with? Why?

2. On a personal level. Ask a classmate to describe the kind of meal he or she really enjoys eating. Ask the same person to describe a meal he or she doesn't enjoy.

4 LANGUAGE STUDY

A. Adjectives Ending in -ed and -ing

disgusted or disgusting? interested or interesting?

1. Study these four sentences. Can you explain the difference between sentences 1 and 2, and between sentences 3 and 4?

1. My parents are disgusting.
2. My parents are disgusted.
3. The students in my class aren't very interested.
4. The students in my class aren't very interesting.

Now find a response (a, b, c, or d) to each of the comments above.

a. Oh? What have you done that upsets them so much?
b. Oh? What do they do that upsets you so much?
c. You mean they don't want to learn anything?
d. You mean you don't enjoy talking to them?

2. Complete these sentences with *disgusted, disgusting, interested,* and *interesting*.

1. The meal I had yesterday was so .... that I don't even want to talk about it.
2. I'm .... with your behavior!
3. Have you read any .... books lately?
4. Are you .... in music?

3. Complete these sentences with the correct form of the verb in parentheses.

1. (*excite*) He will be .... by the news.
2. (*amuse*) She's not an .... person. She's too serious.
3. (*bore*) I'm .... with this TV program. Let's watch something else.
4. (*embarrass*) I've never been so .... in my entire life.
5. (*excite*) My first trip to the United States was ....
6. (*bore*) What a .... movie! Let's leave.
7. (*confuse*) Do you think this exercise is ....?
8. (*amuse*) I don't think the class was .... by my joke.

4. On a personal level. Make sentences about yourself, your family, or your classmates. Use one or two adjectives from each group in the box.

Examples *I'm interested in classical music.*
I think Mozart is especially interesting.

interested (in)	interesting
frightened (by)	frightening
excited (by)	exciting
amused (by)	amusing
challenged (by)	challenging
surprised (by)	surprising
confused (by)	confusing
disgusted (with/by)	disgusting
disappointed (by/in/with)	disappointing
bored (with/by)	boring
exhausted (by)	exhausting
terrified (of/by)	terrifying
fascinated (with/by)	fascinating
embarrassed (by)	embarrassing

B. *I'd rather (not) . . .* and *I'd prefer (not) . . .*

1. Look at these sentences. Can you figure out which ones can be completed with *I'd (I would) rather* and which ones can be completed with *I'd (I would) prefer*? The texts on page 41 might help you.

1. .... to be a vegetarian, but my parents won't let me.
2. .... be a vegetarian, but my parents won't let me.
3. .... not talk about my mother's cooking.
4. .... not to talk about my mother's cooking.
5. I think .... eat at home tonight.
6. Really? Well, I think .... to eat out.

2. Complete these conversations.

Examples A: Do you want to eat out tonight?
B: *(No/eat at home)* No, I'd rather eat at home. **or** No, I'd prefer to eat at home.

A: Do you want to have steak for dinner?
B: *(Yes/be fine)* Yes. That's fine.

1. A: Do you want to invite Tony and Jennifer for dinner?
B: *(No/not have guests tonight)*

2. A: Would you like to go to a movie tonight?
   B: *(Yes/sound good)*
3. A: Do you want to rent a video tonight?
   B: *(No/see that new movie with Kevin Costner)*
4. A: Shall we get something to eat after the movie?
   B: *(Yes/be a good idea)*
5. A: Would you like to go to an Italian restaurant?
   B: *(No/have Chinese food)*
6. A: How about the China Moon then?
   B: *(No/try that new restaurant next to the movie theater)*

C. I'd rather . . . than . . .

1. Look at the list of choices below. You can do one of two things. Which would you rather do? Answer in complete sentences.

Example   Stay home or go dancing
I think I'd rather stay home than go dancing.

1. Watch baseball on television or do something else.
2. Rent a video or go to a movie theater.
3. Go to a party or stay at home and read.
4. Be alone or be with friends.
5. Study English or study another subject.
6. Eat meat or eat vegetables.

2. On a personal level. In a group, decide what you will all do together on Saturday night. You might consider going to one or more places, for example, to dinner, to a movie, or to a disco. Or you might decide to have a party at a classmate's home.

D. Vocabulary Development: *Make* vs. *do*

1. Compare some of the things we do and some of the things we make.

We do:	We make:
• the shopping	• trouble for other people
• the laundry	• a salad for dinner
• homework	• a cake for dessert
• jobs around the house	• a mess
• business	• mistakes
• research	• noise

In general, we use one of these words to talk about actions. We use the other word to talk about the results of actions—something that wasn't there before the action.

1. Which word do you think we use to talk about actions?
2. Which word do we use to talk about the results of those actions?

Remember! This is only a general rule.

2. Complete each of these sentences with *make* or *do*.

1. I have to .... the cooking this evening.
2. I'm going to .... a stew and a nice salad.
3. I have a lot of washing to ....
4. My aunt is going to .... me a sweater for my birthday.
5. How many mistakes did you .... on the last test?
6. A: What are you going to .... tonight?
   B: Nothing much. Maybe watch TV.
7. One of the things I like to .... on vacation is go for long walks.
8. Children, children! Don't .... so much noise!

5 THINKING AND WRITING

A. Reading

Read through this letter, ignoring the missing words. Then do the exercises after you have read it.

> Dear Carol,   June 14
>
> I haven't [1]_____ from you in a long time. It must be almost a year, if not longer. Why don't you ever write? Are you all right? Are you [2]_____ enjoying your job at that advertising agency? Did you get my last letter? I sent it to you in April.
>
> I [3]_____ the last of my final exams yesterday. Of course, I don't have the results [4]_____, but I'm pretty sure I passed them all. In a few weeks, I'll have to start looking for a job. Even with my degree in English and Communications, there's no guarantee that I'll find one. Maybe I should have gotten a job after I finished high school like you did — instead of [5]_____ to college. I won't say I haven't enjoyed the last four years, but to tell you the truth, they haven't been easy! I never had enough money, and I'm up to my ears in debt because I've [6]_____ so much from my parents. Sometimes I wonder if it's really been [7]_____ all the trouble! I mean, what's the point of getting an education if you can't even be sure of getting a job in the end?
>
> Still, I can't really complain. I've [8]_____ lots of friends while I've been here, and this last year has been the best of all. I've been sharing a house with three other students and we take turns [9]_____ the cooking. It's not always terrific, but at least it's a lot better than the awful stuff they serve in the university cafeteria! I've become pretty good at [10]_____ different kinds of vegetarian dishes, mostly with natural rice. You know what I mean? It's the brown kind, not the white variety.
>
> Write and [11]_____ me what you've been doing these past few months. It will be good to hear from you even if it's only a few lines. You can write to me c/o my parents. Here's the address just in case you've forgotten it: 1735 West Roscoe Street, Chicago, Illinois 60657.
>
> Looking [12]_____ to hearing from you soon.
>
> Yours,
> Chris

1. Talk about your impression of Chris. Answer these questions and then give reasons for your answers.

1. Is Chris a man or a woman?
2. How old is he/she?
3. What is Chris's relationship with Carol? For example, are they friends, brother and sister, in love with each other?
4. Imagine a typical day in Chris's life during the past year. Describe some of the things Chris probably did.

2. Here are six of the missing words from the letter. Where do they go?

a. worth   b. making   c. doing   d. yet   e. still
f. forward

What are the other six missing words?

B. Writing

Write a short letter to a friend you haven't heard from for six months. Use any phrases you can from the letter above. Be sure to cover these points:

1. Mention that you wrote a letter six months ago and still haven't gotten an answer.
2. Briefly tell your friend what you have done and have been doing during the past six months.
3. Ask your friend a few questions about things you want to know.
4. Mention something you are looking forward to doing or any plans you have for the future.

UNIT 6 Would You Do This?

1 READING, LISTENING, AND DISCUSSION

A. Discussion

Look at the painting. Then read what the artist had to say about it. What is different about the men in reality and the way the picture was painted?

"I little knew that this picture I painted of the garbage collectors cheerfully getting rid of our garbage would be all that I'd see of them for a month or so, since the next day they all went out on strike. I had to open the back gate for them and liked all the bustle and activity going on, especially with the large rubber gloves. Not *quite* so large or tomato red in reality I suspect."

Beryl Cook

Discuss these questions.
1. Would you like to do this job? Give reasons for your answer.
2. Do you think this is a useful job? Why or why not?
3. Describe some jobs you would not do, and give your reasons.
4. Now talk about some jobs you would like to do. Tell why.

UNIT 6

B. Reading

Read the five parts of the following story. See if you notice anything unusual.

1 The woman gave us a dirty look and closed the door. We stood there in the rain. A minute later the door opened again. This time it was Simmons himself. "Who are you? What do you want?" he shouted at Jane. He hadn't seen me in the dark. "We've been trying to contact you at work for the past three days, Mr. Simmons. But they said you've been sick," I said.

2 "Good evening, Mrs. Simmons. We're looking for your husband," Jane said. "He isn't here," the woman said without even asking who we were. She probably didn't have to. "Yes, he is, Mrs. Simmons. We know he is! Now just tell him we want to talk to him. We're not leaving until we've seen him," Jane told her.

3 Jane's my partner. People can get nasty sometimes in these situations. But Jane isn't easy to scare. She used to be a police officer. She's almost as big as I am and she's just as tough. We rang the bell and waited. A middle-aged woman opened the door and looked at us suspiciously. Probably his wife, I thought.

4 He looked at me and calmed down. Jane told him why we had come. "We can talk out here. But it'd be better if we went inside," I said. He didn't answer for a moment. "I've been expecting this for a long time. I suppose I can't run away from it," he said finally.

5 We had chosen the time carefully. They had just sat down to dinner when we got there. The house was in one of the poorer parts of town. It was a cold, winter evening, around 7 P.M. That's usually the best time to catch them at home. People don't expect us then. "There's his car. And the lights are on inside the house," Jane said.

1. You probably noticed that the five parts of the story are not in the right order. Put them in the order you think is correct.

2. Give your opinion and give reasons for your choice. Do your classmates agree?

1. What kind of work do you think the writer does?
2. What do you think his partner looks like? Try to describe her.
3. Why do you think they wanted to see Simmons?
4. How did Simmons probably feel when he saw them?
   a. Very frightened and surprised
   b. Angry but not very surprised
   c. It is impossible to say.

C. Listening

Listen to an interview with the man in the story. Then answer these questions.

1. What exactly does this man do?
2. Why does he work with a partner?
3. What kind of people does he deal with?
4. How does he feel about his work?
5. Which do you think is probably the better description?
   a. The man takes a personal interest in the people he deals with.
   b. He is not very interested in their personal problems.
   Explain why you think one description is better.

2 LANGUAGE STUDY

A. The Past Perfect (*they had sat down*) and the Simple Past (*they sat down*)

1. Look at the pairs of sentences carefully. Is there an important difference in meaning?

1. They sat down to dinner when we got there.
2. They had sat down to dinner when we got there.

3. I felt sick. I hadn't eaten for ten days.
4. I felt sick. I didn't eat for ten days.

5. When the murderer saw the dead man's wife, he broke down and confessed.
6. When the murderer saw the dead man's wife, he had broken down and confessed.

Look at sentences 1 and 2. Say which action happened first, or before the other one. How do you know? What about the other sentences?

2. Complete these sentences with the Past Perfect (*I'd been/I hadn't been*).

Examples I (*be*) to Canada several times before, but I enjoyed my last trip the most.
I'd been to Canada several times before, but I enjoyed my last trip the most.

Michel (*not be*) to Canada for a long time. It was his first visit in ten years.
Michel hadn't been to Canada for a long time. It was his first visit in ten years.

1. I just returned from a wonderful trip to Canada. I (*go*) there several times before for vacation, but this time was special.
2. For one thing, I (*never be*) to Quebec before.
3. Of course, I (*see*) pictures of its fascinating narrow streets and old houses.
4. And I (*hear*) about its cafes and restaurants.
5. But I (*not think*) about going there—until I met Michel, that is.
6. Michel is from there and six months after I (*meet*) him, we went to Quebec and Montreal on our honeymoon.

3. Which action happened first? Use the Past Perfect (*he'd lived*) and the Simple Past (*he lived*) in each sentence.

I remember a story my dad liked to tell. He (^{1} *live*) and worked in Detroit for thirteen years when he (^{2} *decide*) to move to New York. He (^{3} *move*) because he (^{4} *lose*) his job. He (^{5} *work*) in an automobile factory there for eight years before he (^{6} *be*) fired.

He finally found a job as a garbage collector—or sanitation worker, as they call it in New York. But by the time he (^{7} *find*) work, he (^{8} *use up*) most of his savings and he was pretty depressed. At one point, he (^{9} *not eat*) a good meal in several days and he (^{10} *be*) beginning to feel sick. But after he (^{11} *start*) his new job, he (^{12} *not feel*) so bad. He had money in his pocket again!

4. Read the three parts of the story. Guess what had happened and complete each part.

1. Once, an old woman made a cake, put it in a cake tin, and said, "I won't eat it until Christmas." She had a grandson named Max. Max knew where the cake was. When Christmas came, she opened the tin but the cake wasn't there.
Why not?

2. Years later, when Max was older, he had a job in an office. He owed some gangsters a lot of money and knew that they were coming to the office at 5 o'clock. What do you think he had done when they came?

3. Several years later, in another country, Max had a girlfriend named Nina. Nina had some jewelry that her parents had given her. She kept it in her bedroom. The day after she and Max broke up, she looked for the jewelry but couldn't find it. Can you guess what had happened?

5. On a personal level. Tell your classmates about an exciting or unpleasant thing that happened to you. Say what had happened first.

Example *Once I was out very late and when I got home, the door was open. Someone had gone in and stolen my TV and stereo. I guess it was my own fault in a way. You see, I'd forgotten to lock the door.*

6. Say these sentences aloud.

1. I'd like to see you.
2. I'd rather see you tomorrow.
3. I'd never seen the man before.
4. They'd sat down to dinner when we got there.
5. I'd be in trouble.
6. I'd been in trouble.
7. They'd all go home if they had a chance.
8. They'd all gone home by the time I called.

Explain what the *'d* stands for in each of the sentences above. Then complete these sentences.

9. He .... met me before, but he didn't recognize me.
10. That's a good suggestion, but I think we .... rather eat at home.
11. Why don't you try it? I think you .... like it.
12. I .... be in Los Angeles now if I .... gotten a scholarship to the university there.

B. Pronunciation

1. 📼 Words and Sounds. Listen to these groups of words. Which word does not belong in each group?

1. lam**b**	de**b**t	trou**b**le	bom**b**ing
2. **k**nee	**k**ick	**k**now	**k**nife
3. answer	**w**rite	t**w**o	**w**ith
4. **w**rong	**w**oman	**w**ork	**w**eather
5. fri**gh**t	tou**gh**	li**gh**t	si**gh**t
6. **h**ouse	**h**ome	**h**air	**h**our
7. col**d**	coul**d**	woul**d**	shoul**d**
8. ca**l**m	ta**l**k	wi**l**d	wa**l**k

Pronounce the words aloud. Pay particular attention to the letters in bold.

2. 📼 Stress and Intonation. Listen to these sentences. Then say the sentences aloud, putting stress on the word in bold. How does the meaning change?

Which question do you think means these things?

a. Tell me again what you want. I didn't understand the first time you told me.
b. Well, if you don't want what I thought you wanted, what is it that you want?
c. I know what the other people want. What about you?

3. 📼 Listen to these sentences. Then say the sentences aloud. What do you think they mean?

1. What are you doing **here**?
2. What are you **doing** here?
3. What are **you** doing here?
4. What **are** you doing here?
5. **What** are you doing here?

3 READING AND THINKING

▲ A Discussion

Each of these three people is looking for a job. Study the facts about each person and look at the job advertisements. Then discuss these questions.

1. Which job or jobs do you think each person should apply for? Give reasons.
2. Which job or jobs do you think they should not apply for? Again, give reasons.

Mike Lopez (27)

Now employed as a television repair serviceman but wants something better. Speaks Spanish well. Is a good conversationalist and is very intelligent. Will work long hours but must have weekends free for his family.

Theresa Gower (21)

Has just finished college with a degree in Mathematics. Would like a job involving scientific research. Studied French in high school. Can drive and has a pleasant, outgoing personality. Is willing to do anything for a few months as long as it is interesting. Likes animals.

Carol Simpson (21)

Graduated from high school at 18 with good grades in all subjects, especially math and science. Now works as a receptionist for an advertising agency but doesn't find it very interesting. Gets along well with all kinds of people and would like to travel.

Personal Companion
Wealthy, eccentric writer, 68, seeks young, attractive traveling companion and personal secretary, 18–30. Must have warm, cheerful personality. Opportunity to visit Europe and Japan and meet interesting people. 263-7693. Ask for Mrs. Arden.

Kitchen Staff for Hotel
Summer positions available for assistant chefs and experienced kitchen help. Good salary. Shift work (6AM–2PM or 3PM–11PM). Call 629-7748 ext. 110.

Collection Agency
Seeks men or women willing to work evenings. Knowledge of karate or other self-defense skills useful. Good salary for the right person. Call 257-3636 between 9:00 and 5:00 Mon.–Sat.

Good with Animals?
Young person 18–25 wanted for work in animal hospital. Must be able to handle dogs, cats, birds, snakes, and other pets. Job includes some clerical work. Must have driver's license. Call 935-2201.

WANT TO BE RICH?
New, expanding company seeks Management Trainees. Good salary and benefits. Excellent opportunities for promotion and advancement. Must be ambitious with good communication skills. Knowledge of French or Spanish a plus but not essential. No previous experience necessary. Call now at 439-2208.

▼ B. On a Personal Level

1. If you had only these jobs to choose from, which of them would you apply for? Why?
2. Is there a job you would not apply for? Give reasons.
3. What kind of work do you actually do now?
4. If you could start over again (in other words, if you could be or do anything you wanted), would you do the same kind of work or would you choose a different occupation? Why? (If you don't work, tell about a job that interests you.)

4 LANGUAGE STUDY

A. Impersonal *they*

1. Compare the sentences in each pair.

1. They offered me a good salary and excellent benefits.
2. I was offered a good salary and excellent benefits.
3. They make trucks and farm equipment there.
4. Trucks and farm equipment are made there.
5. They say that they are going to build two new factories.
6. The people I've met say that two new factories are going to be built.

In sentences 1, 3, and 5, does *they* mean a or b?

a. people mentioned to the reader or listener before
b. people it is not really important to name or describe

Which of the sentences above (1–6) seem a little more formal—in other words, the kind you would use in a written or oral report, a newspaper article, or a job application?

2. Pretend that you have to make a formal speech in English about an important city in your country. Use the more formal passive construction rather than the informal *they*.

Example They've made a number of changes here recently.
A number of changes have been made here recently.

1. They're going to hold the Olympic Games here next year.
2. They expect thousands of visitors from all over the world.
3. They've built three new hotels.
4. They'll finish two more this year.
5. They've already improved the public transportation system.
6. They opened a new airport last month.
7. When they chose this city for the Olympic Games, they had already planned many of these things.
8. Now they've already done many of them.

3. On a personal level. Give a short formal speech. Talk about three or four changes that have been made recently in a city you know.

1. First, make notes, following the examples in Exercise 2 (They've made a number of changes in .... recently.).
2. Then make your speech using the passive construction.

B. The Causative: Having Things Done

1. Which sentences mean *This is not something I do or did myself*?

1. I washed these clothes at the hotel.
2. I had these clothes washed at the hotel.
3. I repaired the television set.
4. I had the television set repaired.
5. I cut my hair every six weeks.
6. I have my hair cut every six weeks.

Explain how you know that some of the sentences mean *I don't/didn't do this myself*.

2. Complete these sentences with the correct form of *have* and the verb in parentheses.

1. This sweater has a stain on it. Where can I .... it ....? (clean)
2. My car broke down yesterday and it will cost a lot to .... it .... (repair)
3. The President .... his picture .... by several famous artists. (paint)
4. She's very rich and always .... all her clothes .... in Paris. (make)
5. I took some pictures, but after I .... them ...., I found they weren't very good. (develop)
6. This room looks awfully shabby. Why don't you .... it .... if you can't do it yourself? (paint)

▶ UNIT 6

Mrs. Arden (68)

3. Mrs. Arden, who wrote one of the ads on page 49, has hired a personal companion. What she is telling her new companion is wrong because Mrs. Arden never does anything herself. What are the correct sentences?

Example I want you to learn how I do everything.
I want you to learn how I have everything done.

1. I serve my breakfast every morning at 6 o'clock.
2. I will serve your breakfast at the same time.
3. I've cooked my eggs the same way for forty years.
4. I will prepare your eggs the same way tomorrow.
5. I washed my laundry yesterday before you arrived.
6. In the future, I can do your laundry with mine.
7. I cleaned your room this morning.
8. I've taken your suitcase to your room.
9. After you get settled, there are some letters I'd like to type.
10. And then, this afternoon, I have to cut my hair.

4. On a Personal Level

1. Name two things you have done for you regularly now.
2. Name one thing you've had someone else do for you all your life.
3. Name two things you hate doing that you'd like to have done for you.

▼ C. Vocabulary Development

1. Which word do you need to complete each sentence?

earn or *win*?
1. You can .... lots of prizes in this contest.
2. How much money do you .... in your job?

lend or *borrow*?
3. Can you .... me some money until tomorrow?
4. I didn't have enough money, so I had to .... some from a friend.

spend or *save*?
5. I'm trying to .... enough money so that I can buy a car.
6. How much money do you .... on food and other essentials?

price or *cost*?
7. The .... of gas has gone up again.
8. The .... of living has gone up again.

2. Answer these questions alone. Then compare your answers with your classmates.

1. A profession is some kind of work that
   a. requires special training and education.
   b. pays very well.
   c. anyone can do.

2. The staff of a company is made up of
   a. ordinary workers.
   b. management.
   c. both a and b.

3. What do many people hope to do after working for many years?
   a. Die
   b. Work harder
   c. Retire

4. What do we call the money people get after they retire?
   a. Rent
   b. A pension
   c. A salary

5. Your employer is
   a. the work you do.
   b. the person you work for.
   c. both a and b.

6. An employee is
   a. someone who has a nice, clean job.
   b. someone who gives work to other people.
   c. anyone who works for someone else.

7. Which one of these would you write if a company wanted to know about your education and experience?
   a. A résumé
   b. A biography
   c. A history of life

8. After you write it, you should send it to the .... department.
   a. personal
   b. personality
   c. personnel

5 WRITING AND LISTENING

A. Writing

1. This is a letter of application for one of the jobs advertised on page 49. Eight words are missing. Here are six of the words. Where do they belong?

a. graduated b. give c. apply
d. available e. for f. Sincerely

What are the other two missing words in the letter?

> Dear Sir or Madam:
>
> I would like to ¹_____ for the job that was advertised in yesterday's Evening Post.
> I ²_____ from high school last year. My best subjects were English, Math, Computer Science and Spanish. Since I graduated, I have had several part-³_____ jobs, including one as a computer operator for an international travel company. Unfortunately, that job was only ⁴_____ the summer.
> I ⁵_____ to find a full-time job that offers management training and opportunities for promotion. I am sure that my previous employers will ⁶_____ me good references.
> I am ⁷_____ for an interview at your convenience.
>
> ⁸_____ yours,

2. Which of the jobs on page 49 do you think this person is applying for?

3. Choose one of the jobs advertised on page 49 and write a letter of application. Be sure to mention:

1. information about school.
2. previous work experience or other experience you think may help you get the job.
3. any special qualifications you have.
4. anything else you think should be in the letter.

B. Listening

1. This is a version of a popular game called *20 Questions*. A team of three people has to find out what a person's job is.

Here are the rules: The team has to find out the person's job within a total of 20 questions. All questions must be the kind that can be answered with *Yes* or *No*.

Here are the questions a team asked one person:

Q: Are any special qualifications or training necessary for this job?
A: No. Not really.
Q: Does that mean anybody can do it?
A: Uh... no, that's not true either.
Q: Do men do this job too?
A: Yes, sometimes.
Q: Is this the kind of job people usually do in an office?
A: No.
Q: Well, could you do this job at home?
A: No.
Q: Do you travel a lot?
A: Yes.
Q: When you travel, do you usually go by train?
A: No, not by train.
Q: By plane?
A: Yes.
Q: Hmm... do you usually wear a uniform?
A: No.

Can you guess what the person's job is?

2. 🔊 Listen to the team's questions and to the woman's answers. Then answer these questions.

1. Does the woman travel by herself?
2. What exactly does the woman do?
3. As you listened, what were your impressions of the woman? Her age, nationality, personality, etc.?

3. On a personal level. Form two or more teams. Each team chooses a job and discusses the description of that job. Then one team asks questions and tries to guess the other team's job. Whichever team gets the answer with the fewest questions wins!

LANGUAGE SUMMARY FOR UNIT 5

1. Using the Passive Voice

Potatoes were discovered in Peru in the 1500s.
They were discovered by the Spaniards.
Today, potatoes are eaten in many countries around the world.
They can be cooked in many different ways.
In some countries, they used to be eaten raw.

2. Using the correct adjective: *-ed* or *-ing*

The students in my class aren't very interested in learning English.
The students in my class aren't very interesting, so I don't talk to them very much.
The meal I had yesterday was so disgusting that I don't even want to think about it.
I'm disgusted with your behavior!

3. Expressing preference with *I'd rather (not)* and *I'd prefer (not)*

I'd prefer to be a vegetarian, but my parents won't let me.
I'd rather be a vegetarian, but my parents won't let me.
I think I'd rather stay home than go dancing.

4. Vocabulary Development

Methods of cooking: *roast, bake, fry, boil, broil, grill*

A leg of lamb is usually roasted in the oven.
Bread is baked in an oven.
French fries are long, thin slices of potato that are fried.
What is one of the most common ways to cook vegetables? Boil them in water.
The Americans are famous for their broiled steaks.
Some people grill hamburgers or steak outdoors.

Make and *do*

I have to do the cooking this evening.
I'm going to make a stew and a nice salad.
I'm going to do my homework after school.
How many mistakes did you make on the last test?

5. Pronunciation: Words and Sounds

peas   bread
bread   pepper   lean
bean   beef   pear
beef   meal   pizza   beer
fish   ripe
cake   steak   veal

LANGUAGE SUMMARY FOR UNIT 6

1. Saying what happened first with the Past Perfect

I'd been to Canada several times before, but I enjoyed this trip the most.
By the time he found work, he'd used up most of his savings.

2. Understanding what *'d* means

I'd like to see you. (*would*)
I'd rather see you tomorrow. (*would*)
I'd never seen the man before. (*had*)

3. Using the impersonal *they*

They offered me a good salary and excellent benefits.
They make trucks and farm equipment there for export.
They say that they are going to build two new factories.

4. Using the Passive Voice in formal situations

A number of changes have been made here recently.
The Olympic Games are going to be held here next year.
Thousands of visitors are expected from all over the world.

5. Using the Causative: Having things done

I had my clothes washed yesterday.
You can have your laundry done when they do mine.
I have my hair cut every six weeks.
I've had my hair cut at the same place for twenty years.

6. Vocabulary Development

earn—win   spend—save
lend—borrow   price—cost

7. Pronunciation

Words and Sounds:

de**b**t	**t**rouble	li**gh**t	**t**ough
know	**k**ick	**h**ouse	**h**our
write	**w**ith	coul**d**	col**d**
wrong	**w**oman	tal**k**	wil**d**

Stress and Intonation:
What do you **want**?
What do **you** want?
What **do** you want?
What do you want?

UNIT 7 Are They Crazy or Am I?

1 READING AND THINKING

A. Pre-reading

Look at the picture. Can you answer these questions without reading the text?

1. What was this man's name?
2. Why was he famous?
3. What else do you know about him?

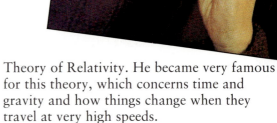

B. Reading

Keep the questions above in mind as you read this biographical sketch.

He was one of the greatest scientists and thinkers in history. However, he was not considered very bright when he was a child. When he was nine, his father told his mother he was very worried about him because he was "a little slow." His teachers complained that he had no sense of discipline and that he was a bad influence on the other students.

When he was fifteen, he was thrown out of school, but a few years later he was allowed to study mathematics and physics at a special technical university in Zurich. But even at the university, he was hardly "a good student." He rarely attended classes, and he was often in trouble with his professors because he constantly argued with them. One of them told him: "You're smart; extremely smart. But you have one real fault; you never let yourself be told anything!"

When he graduated from the university, he couldn't get a job—partly because none of his professors would recommend him for one. Finally, he found one in the Swiss Patent Office in Berne. One of his duties was writing descriptions of new inventions. This helped him learn how to write clearly and simply. He later said that the only thing that made many problems in science seem difficult was the language they were described in.

In 1905, when he was only twenty-six, he published an article in a scientific journal. The article dealt with a theory which he called the Theory of Relativity. He became very famous for this theory, which concerns time and gravity and how things change when they travel at very high speeds.

All his life, he lived very simply and was totally uninterested in money, power, or fame. He could never understand why so many people admired him and wanted to meet him. He knew that most of them had never read anything he had written and that they didn't understand his ideas. "Are they crazy or am I?" he asked.

1. Find the words in the text that mean:

1. smart, quick at learning things
2. not very smart or quick at learning things
3. not often at all
4. very often; again and again
5. to get a degree and leave a school
6. a part of the government that gives people the right to make and sell new inventions
7. the force or pull that one object, such as a planet, has on a smaller object, such as the moon

2. Give your opinion. Do your classmates agree?

1. Is there anything about the man's childhood that surprises you?
2. Do you think he was very popular with his professors at the university? Give reasons for your answer.
3. He later said that his time at the Swiss Patent Office was one of the most important periods of his life. Why do you think he said this?
4. Do you think Einstein was crazy?

2 LANGUAGE STUDY

A. Vocabulary Development: Words That Describe Intelligence

1. Which of the words below would you like other people to use about you? Which would you not like other people to use about you? Why?

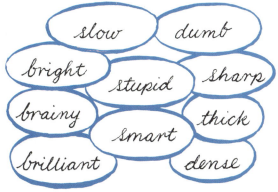

slow, dumb, bright, stupid, sharp, brainy, thick, smart, brilliant, dense

2. Divide the words above into two groups. One group means more or less the same as *intelligent*. How would you label the other group?

B. Pronunciation: Words and Sounds

Is it thick or sick?

1. Listen to these words. Which one do you hear? Is it in column A or in column B?

A	B
thick	sick
think	sink
thin	sin
thumb	sum
thigh	sigh
thought	sought
theories	series
thing	sing

Now practice saying the words.

2. Repeat these questions aloud. Then close your book and ask a classmate at least three of the questions you have just repeated. Listen carefully to the answer. Is it an answer to the question you asked?

1. Are you thick?
2. Are you sick?
3. Do you ever think when you take a bath?
4. Do you ever sink when you take a bath?
5. Can you say the word *thing*?
6. Can you say the word *sing*?

C. The Definite Article *the*

1. What's the difference between sentences 1 and 2, and between sentences 3 and 4?

1. She isn't interested in marriage.
2. She isn't interested in the marriage.
3. Do you like music?
4. Do you like the music?

Which sentence above means:

a. Do you like the music you can hear now?
b. She isn't interested in getting married. She likes being single.

What do the other two sentences mean?

2. Match the beginning of the sentence on the left with its appropriate ending on the right.

1. I want the money
2. I want money
3. I've always been interested in science
4. I've always been interested in the science
5. I'm not interested in theory
6. I know very little about the Theory
7. Gravity
8. The gravity

a. and I don't care whose it is or how I get it.
b. I lent you last week.
c. and mathematics in general.
d. of management, although some people prefer to call it an art.
e. of Relativity.
f. for its own sake; I'm only interested when it becomes useful in some way.
g. of the moon is not very strong.
h. is one of the most powerful forces we know.

▶ UNIT 7

3. Complete these paragraphs with *the* when it is necessary.

¹............ word *science* refers to many fields of study. For example, it refers to ²............ biology, ³............ anatomy, ⁴............ chemistry, ⁵............ physics, and ⁶............ astronomy. These fields of science can be broken down further. For example, there is ⁷............ anatomy of plants and ⁸............ anatomy of animals. ⁹............ study of one or more of these subjects may lead to a special career. ¹⁰............ doctors, for example, study such things as ¹¹............ physiology and ¹²............ anatomy of human beings. ¹³............ engineers and architects need a knowledge of ¹⁴............ physics.

¹⁵............ students in my class are all interested in science. They want to be ¹⁶............ doctors, nurses, and engineers. ¹⁷............ only student who is not interested in ¹⁸............ science wants to be an artist.

D. Adverbs and Expressions of Frequency

1. In each of the sentences below, there is a word or phrase that tells you how often something happens. Find it and put it in the correct category in the chart.

a. Often or more than often	b. Sometimes	c. Less than sometimes

1. He hardly ever attended classes.
2. He was constantly in trouble.
3. He occasionally did some experiments.
4. I read books about science now and then.
5. I seldom watch television.
6. I frequently listen to the radio.
7. She phones me once in a while.
8. I go jogging regularly.

2. Put the adverbs in parentheses in the correct place in the sentences.

Examples (*constantly*) He was in trouble.
He was constantly in trouble.

(*always*) He has been an independent thinker.
He has always been an independent thinker.

1. School is hard. (*hardly ever*) I have any free time.
2. (*always*) I'm studying.
3. (*seldom*) I have a date or take a break.
4. (*never*) My classes are easy.
5. (*frequently*) My assignments are very difficult.
6. (*always*) I can't understand them.
7. (*always*) I have been pretty smart.
8. (*frequently*) But now I have to get help.
9. (*usually*) Fortunately, I pass my exams.
10. (*occasionally*) However, I fail one.

3. Look at these sentences. Some adverbs—especially adverbs that end in *-ly*—can be used in more than one place in a sentence. Where? Where can you use phrases such as *now and then*?

1. Occasionally, we take a break from our studies.
2. We occasionally take a break from our studies.
3. We take a break from our studies occasionally.
4. Now and then, I have a date.
5. I have a date now and then.

4. Make at least two different sentences using the adverbs and phrases in parentheses.

1. (*frequently*) I visit science museums.
2. (*sometimes*) I stay in a museum for several hours.
3. (*once in a while*) I go to an international science conference.
4. And (*occasionally*) I read science magazines.
5. (*now and then*) I even write an article for one of these magazines.
6. But (*usually*) they don't accept what I write.

5. On a personal level. Interview a classmate and take notes. Find out how often your classmate does these things.

1. watch television
2. eat foreign food
3. go out at night
4. get exercise or play a sport
5. use an English dictionary
6. listen to radio programs in English

Make sentences about the person you interviewed, using adverbs and expressions of frequency. Report your findings to the class.

3 READING, LISTENING, AND DISCUSSION

A. Reading

Read this conversation. One of the speakers is a mother. Who do you think the other speaker is? Why?

A: Now, then, Mrs. Rider . . . what seems to be the problem?
B: Well, I just can't . . . can't sleep at night. I just lie awake worrying.
A: What about?
B: Well . . . it's my son . . . David. He's only twelve years old, but he's so . . . so different.
A: Different?
B: Yes . . . different . . . strange . . . He isn't like other kids his age . . .
A: What do you mean?
B: Well . . . uh . . . all he ever does is read books about Albert Einstein . . . It's all he ever talks about. It's always Einstein said this and Einstein did that. He's always talking about him . . . about how he was the greatest scientist who ever lived, the greatest thinker there ever was, and on and on and on. He never stops!
A: You mean, he gets on your nerves sometimes?
B: Yes. I mean, wouldn't he get on yours, too?
A: Yes, I suppose he would. How's he doing at school?
B: Well, the teachers say that he's one of the brightest students there when it comes to math, but that he isn't interested in any other subject. And he has a lot of trouble with the other kids . . . they call him "nerd" and "four-eyes." They don't like him at all.
A: Why?
B: He's always using long words they don't understand . . . even I don't understand them sometimes. He has a very big vocabulary for someone his age.
A: Well, that isn't such a bad thing, is it?
B: No . . . no, I suppose not, but I just wish he weren't so . . . so nervous all the time.
A: Nervous? How do you mean?
B: Always talking all the time, always about the same things . . . I was wondering if you could . . . could help somehow?
A: Help? Who? Him or you?

Discuss these questions.

1. Explain what David does that gets on his mother's nerves.
2. What is it about him that other children don't like?
3. If you were the other person in the conversation, what advice would you give Mrs. Rider?

B. Listening

▶ **Listen to the whole conversation on cassette. You will hear some things that are not in the text.**

1. Discuss these questions.

1. As you listened, did you get any idea of the room Mrs. Rider was in? If so, describe what you would probably see if you were in it.
2. Where did you think the other person probably was and what was she doing during the conversation?
3. What do you think the other person was going to give Mrs. Rider before she left?

2. On a personal level. Talk about what you were like when you were David's age. These questions might help you.

1. Were you similar in any way to David?
2. What were you interested in at that time?
3. How did you feel about school?

C. Pronunciation: Stress and Intonation

1. ▶ **Listen to this conversation. Then read it aloud.**

A: Does he get on your nerves sometimes?
B: Yes, he does. Wouldn't he get on **yours**, too?

2. Now read these conversations aloud. Which words should be stressed?

A: Is this your book?
B: No. I think it's yours.

A: This is my coat.
B: No, it isn't. It's mine!

A: We can't have the party at our place.
B: No? Well, let's have it at ours, then.

▶ **Listen to the conversations and check your answers.**

4 LANGUAGE STUDY

A. Relative Clauses with *who*, *which*, and *that*

1. Study these sentences. When do we use *who* and when do we use *which*?

1. Einstein, who won the Nobel Prize for physics in 1921, was a brilliant man.
2. The Theory of Relativity, which concerns time and gravity and how things change when they travel at high speeds, made him famous.

Can we use *that* instead of *which* or *who* in the sentences above? What about in the sentences below?

3. Most people don't understand the work which was done by Einstein.
4. I've never met anyone who is as important as Einstein.

2. Complete these sentences with *who*, *which*, or *that*.

1. My son, David, ... is only twelve years old, is very interested in Albert Einstein.
2. Einstein was a scientist .... was born in 1879.
3. He was born in Ulm, ... is a small city in Germany.
4. He later studied at the Swiss Federal Polytechnic School in Zurich, ... at that time was one of the most famous universities in the world.
5. He is famous now for a theory .... has changed our concepts of time, space, and the universe.
6. This theory, ... is called the Theory of Relativity, was first published in 1905.
7. Later in his life, thousands of people .... didn't understand his ideas wanted to meet him.
8. Einstein, ... died in 1955, once asked, "Are they crazy or am I?"

In which sentence above can you use either *that* or *which*? In which sentence can you use either *that* or *who*?

3. Look at what this doctor wrote about Anna Lopez. The doctor could improve his writing style if he used relative pronouns (*who*, *which*, *that*). Join sentences 1–2, 3–4, 5–6, 7–8, 9–10, 11–12, and 13–14.

Examples (1–2) *I've just interviewed Anna Lopez, who is an extremely intelligent child.*

(3–4) *Unfortunately, Anna's school, which is near my office, does not specialize in the education of gifted children.*

¹I've just interviewed Anna Lopez. ²Anna Lopez is an extremely intelligent child. ³Unfortunately, Anna's school does not specialize in the education of gifted children. ⁴Anna's school is near my office.
⁵Anna's mother thinks she is a strange girl. ⁶Anna's mother is concerned about her. ⁷Anna understands words and concepts. ⁸These words and concepts are incomprehensible to the average adult. ⁹She reads books about such things as chemistry and physics. ¹⁰Chemistry and physics are very difficult subjects for a young child. ¹¹However, Anna is very gifted for a child. ¹²The child is only ten years old. ¹³Someday she will probably make a discovery or write a book. ¹⁴The discovery or book will make her famous.

B. The Superlative of Adjectives

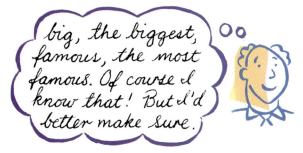

Complete these sentences with the correct form of the word in parentheses.

Examples New York is one of (*big*) cities in the world.
New York is one of the biggest cities in the world.

It is also one of (*exciting*).
It is also one of the most exciting.

1. When he was a child in school, Einstein did not appear to be one of (*bright*) students.
2. However, today many people feel Einstein was (*great*) scientist who ever lived.
3. It is certainly true that his Theory of Relativity is one of (*important*) concepts in science.
4. This theory helps us understand how even (*small*) things in the universe behave.
5. Some of (*famous*) people in the world wanted to meet him.
6. A photographer once said that Einstein had one of (*interesting*) faces he had ever seen.
7. Einstein spent his last years at one of (*good*) universities in the United States.
8. He believed that one of (*bad*) things he had ever done was to help develop the atomic bomb.
9. Is this one of (*easy*) exercises you have ever done?
10. I hope it isn't (*difficult*).

C. Vocabulary Development

1. Change the form of the word in *italics* so that it fits the sentence. Use *-er, -or,* or *-ist*.

1. *act* — James Dean was a famous ....
2. *science* — Einstein was a great ....
3. *biology* — My sister is a ....
4. *chemistry* — I wanted to become a ....
5. *murder* — I told you it was an accident. I'm not a ....!
6. *psychology* — I'm a .... who works with gifted children.
7. *ideal* — Most young people are ....
8. *direct* — The .... of Personnel is here to see you.

2. For each category, make a list of other nouns that describe people or their professions. Think of as many as you can.

-er	-or	-ist

Do any of these words above come from other nouns or verbs that you know?

3. *Always* sometimes means *too often* or "it's getting on my nerves." Which of these sentences complain about something that gets on someone's nerves?

1. I always get up at around seven.
2. You're always coming late!
3. David is always talking about Einstein.
4. The sun always rises in the east and sets in the west.

Look again at the sentences above. Is there anything in those sentences besides the word *always* that suggests *too often* or "it's getting on my nerves"?

4. How can you say these things with *always*?

1. You make that mistake much too often.
2. You criticize me much too often.
3. You tell the same jokes much too often.
4. You borrow things much too often.
5. I lose my temper much too often.
6. This machine breaks down much too often.

D. Pronunciation: Words and Sounds

1. 📼 Listen to these groups of words. Then pronounce them. In which groups does the sound *ch* change? In which two groups is there no change?

1. charge   change   champagne
2. chair   charm   character
3. channel   chaos   chapter
4. check   chef   chest
5. check   cheese   chemistry
6. choose   chop   chorus
7. China   Chinese   chicken
8. Chile   chili   child

2. 📼 Pronounce the words in column A. Then pronounce the ones in column B. Next, listen and decide if you hear a word from column A or column B.

A	B
cheap, chair	sheep, share
choose, chips	shoes, ships
cheese, watch	she's, wash
I watched it.	I washed it.

Say a word from one of the columns. Can other people in the class guess if it is in column A or B?

5 THINKING, LISTENING, AND WRITING

▲ A. Questionnaire

When Einstein was a young man, he was considered to be very shy and introverted. What about you? Are you like Einstein, or the opposite (extroverted)? Complete the questionnaire and find out!

ARE YOU INTROVERTED OR EXTROVERTED?

Answer these questions with a simple *Yes* or *No*. Don't think about the questions too long! Just give the first answer that comes into your head.

1. Do you usually feel well and healthy?
2. Do you find it difficult to introduce yourself to strangers at parties?
3. When you buy things, do you find it easy to spend your money without thinking too much about it?
4. Do you sometimes make a fool of yourself and not worry about it later?
5. If you have a problem, do you find it easy to turn to other people for advice?
6. Would you prefer to play the trumpet rather than the flute?
7. Are you always in a hurry, even if you have enough time?
8. Do you often put things off; that is, do them later rather than immediately?
9. Would you prefer to spend your vacation in a city with lots of bright lights rather than in a quiet place in the country?
10. If you saw a famous person in the street, would you find it easy to go up and start a conversation?
11. Generally speaking, do you make up your mind easily when sudden decisions have to be made?
12. Do you often forget things?
13. Do you enjoy doing crossword puzzles?
14. Could you get yourself ready to go to a party in fifteen minutes if you suddenly got an invitation to one?
15. Do you consider yourself more reserved and shy than most people?
16. Do you usually prefer writing letters to making phone calls to people?
17. Do you usually look forward to doing things you have never done before?
18. Do you find it exciting to watch competitive sports such as soccer, baseball, and tennis?
19. Do you often find yourself doing several things at once rather than one thing at a time?
20. Do you often find it difficult to relax, even when you have no work to do?
21. Do you lose your temper easily?
22. Do you usually find it easy to concentrate on something for a long time?
23. Are you often late?
24. Do you—or would you—find it interesting to spend a lot of time doing research and getting information?
25. Do you smile easily and freely?
26. Do you ever find it exciting to take risks even when they are not really necessary?
27. Are you easily bored by dull, routine work or jobs?
28. Do you enjoy gambling?
29. Do you consider yourself reliable?
30. Which do you think would make a better pet, a dog or a cat?

How to find your score

Start out with a score of 30 before you begin. Except for questions 13, 15, and 24, add one point to this score for every question that you answered *Yes*. For questions 13, 15, and 24, subtract one point for each *Yes*. For question 30, if you answered *dog*, add one point. If you answered *cat*, subtract one point.

What the scores mean

49–58 You seem to be very extroverted. You probably find it very difficult to be alone. Other people might feel that you are someone who always has to be the center of attention. This may make it difficult for some people to appreciate you.

38–48 You don't fall easily into either category. Some people may think you are extroverted and not realize your need for space and time of your own. On the whole, however, you are probably very well-balanced. You find it easy to be with people but also like your own company.

25–37 You tend to be more of an introvert than an extrovert. Although you have some very good friends, you probably prefer small groups to large ones. People may sometimes confuse your sensitivity and understanding of other people with reserve or aloofness.

12–24 You are definitely introverted. However, maybe you lack self-confidence. It is this lack of self-confidence that may prevent you from enjoying life to the fullest. There is also a strong possibility that you spend too much time worrying about things which are really not as important as they seem.

Under 12 It would seem that you are extremely shy and lack self-confidence.

Michio Ogawa

Carol Simpson

Maria Silva

B. Reading

The three people shown in the pictures were asked these same two questions:

1. Describe the kind of people you enjoy spending time with. For example, what kind of person or people would you choose to go on vacation with? Or imagine you had to share a house or an apartment with two or three people. What personal qualities should they have?
2. Now describe the kind of people you don't enjoy spending time with. What are the characteristics these people have that you don't like?

Here is what two of the people said. Can you guess who is speaking?

1 "I like people who have the same interests as I do. These people usually enjoy good food and good company. And they are usually pretty easygoing. That is, they are tolerant of other people with different ideas about life and things. They usually enjoy a good discussion or even an argument. They don't mind if other people have completely different opinions from theirs as long as they are willing to discuss those opinions calmly. On the other hand, I don't like people who don't take care of themselves or who smoke. And I don't get along with people who are very sloppy or selfish. For example, a friend of mine came to stay with me once and left her clothes all over my apartment. And she never offered to help with the dishes after I'd cooked for her. Once, when we went out for dinner, she expected me to pay! She wasn't a friend after that. That's the kind of person I don't like!"

2 "I like people who are in good health and who are active, but who don't worry about their health or what they eat all the time. I like people who have the same political views as I do, and who don't argue with me all the time. In fact, I can't stand people who argue all the time, especially if they are arguing with me! And I don't like people who get upset or angry just because someone else smokes. I was at a party recently, and after we had a wonderful meal, I took out a cigarette. The woman who was sitting next to me suddenly turned and said, 'I hope you aren't going to light that!' That's the kind of person I don't like!"

C. Listening

🔊 Listen as one of the three people describes a vacation she spent with two other people. Then answer these questions.

1. What kind of vacation was it?
2. Who were the other people?
3. What did the speaker find out about one of the other people?

D. Writing

1. Interview your classmates.

1. Find out the kind of people they like to spend time with. Get them to describe the qualities or characteristics such people have.
2. Also find out the kind of people they don't like to spend time with. Get them to tell you exactly what such people do that they don't like.

2. In a short composition of two paragraphs, answer the same two questions above for yourself.

1. Describe the kind of people you like to spend time with.
2. Then describe the kind of people you don't like to spend time with, and some of the things they do that you don't like.

UNIT 8 Sunday in the Park

1 READING, THINKING, AND LISTENING

A. Reading

Read the first part of these conversations (1–8). Can you find the second part of each conversation (a–h)?

1. Mommy, can we go to the Natural History Museum now? I want to see that dinosaur again.
2. Well, what would you do if you were me, then? I mean, just what do you expect me to do?
3. Look! That guy is stealing that man's wallet.
4. What would your father do if he found out about us?
5. Then everybody started screaming and shouting and the smoke got thicker and thicker.
6. You should do it too. You'd enjoy your vacation much more if you knew at least a little Spanish.
7. It's about Greta Garbo. Do you know who she was?
8. It says here that in a hundred years people will be living until they're 140 or even 160.

a. Are you sure? What do you think we ought to do?
b. What's the point? Everybody there speaks English anyway, don't they? Besides, I'm too busy.
c. You must have been terrified. What happened then?
d. It all sounds fascinating. But we won't be around then, will we?
e. I don't know! It's your decision, not mine! But I know one thing: if you do it, it'll be the end of our relationship!
f. Let's see . . . uh . . . she was a famous movie star once, wasn't she?
g. He'd be very angry, and you might even lose your job.
h. All right, if that's what you want to do this afternoon.

Now look at the picture. Can you figure out which conversation belongs to which group of people?

B. Listening

You will hear more of one of these conversations. Listen to it and then answer these questions.

1. Which people in the picture do you think are talking?
2. Both speakers use the phrase "this job." Explain what they mean.
3. Explain what the problem is.

2 LANGUAGE STUDY

A. The Conditional (*I would go if...*) in Present Hypothetical Situations

1. Study these sentences, paying special attention to the words in bold. Then decide what the sentences mean, a or b.

1. I **would go** to the park **if** I **had** time.
   a. I don't have time, so it isn't possible to go to the park.
   b. I have time, so it's possible to go to the park.
2. He**'d visit** you in New York next year **if** he **saved** enough money.
   a. He probably will save enough money to visit you in New York.
   b. He probably won't save enough money to visit you in New York.

2. Choose the best way to complete these sentences.

1. What do you think the man would do if he .... someone was trying to pick his pocket?
   a. would know   b. knows   c. knew
2. What would you do if such a thing .... to you?
   a. happened   b. would happen   c. happens
3. In other words, what would you do if someone .... to pick your pocket?
   a. tries   b. would try   c. tried
4. Suppose you .... something like this in a store. What would you do?
   a. see   b. saw   c. would see
5. Or what if you were on a crowded street and you suddenly .... someone shouting "Stop, thief!"
   a. will hear   b. heard   c. would hear
6. Then suppose a young man suddenly .... towards you with two police officers behind him.
   a. would run   b. will run   c. ran
7. What would you do if the police officers were too slow and .... catch him?
   a. can't   b. couldn't   c. wouldn't
8. .... to stop him?
   a. Did you try   b. Would you try   c. Will you try
9. Or .... nothing?
   a. did you do   b. would you do   c. will you do
10. I certainly hope you .... something!
    a. 'd do   b. did   c. will do

3. Complete these conversations with the Conditional (*I'd invite*) and the Simple Past (*I invited*).

Example   A: Are you busy next Sunday?
B: Yes, I am. It's my aunt's birthday.
A: Oh. If you (*not be*) busy, I (*invite*) you to go on a picnic.
Oh. If you weren't busy, I'd invite you to go on a picnic.

1. A: Did I tell you I have a date on Saturday?
   B: No, you didn't. I thought we (*go*) to the park if you (*not have*) anything to do.
   A: Sorry, I can't. I'm going to a movie with Tony.
2. A: Are you sure you don't want anything else?
   B: No, thank you. I've had too much already. If I (*eat*) like this every day, I (*get*) fat.
   A: OK, but I wouldn't want you to get hungry later.
3. A: I can't do this exercise.
   B: Why don't you ask for help? I'm sure the teacher (*explain*) it if you (*ask*) her.
   A: You're probably right.
4. A: Let's go to the beach.
   B: Oh, I don't know. I think my teacher (*be*) upset if I (*miss*) a day of class.
   A: Oh, come on. You can call one of your classmates for the homework assignment.
5. A: .... you (*go*) to the beach with me if I (*tell*) you how much I loved you?
   B: Well, if you put it that way...
   A: Great. I knew you (*change*) your mind if I (*try*) hard enough.
6. A: You know, you (*make*) your parents very happy if you (*call*) them once in a while.
   B: Do you think so?
   A: I know so. You haven't called them in over a month, and they're worried about you.

4. On a personal level. In pairs or groups, discuss what you would do in one of the situations below. If you don't agree with a classmate or have an alternative suggestion, you can say *If I were you, I'd . . .*

Example A: If I saw someone stealing someone else's wallet, I'd try to stop him.
 B: That could be dangerous. If I were you, I'd call the police.
 A: Yes. Maybe you're right.

1. You saw someone in a crowded store putting his hand in someone else's pocket.
2. A rich aunt or uncle died and left you a very large sum of money.
3. You heard a neighbor shouting "Help! Help!" in the middle of the night.
4. You were in class taking a big test, and you started to feel very sick.

B. Pronunciation

1. Words and Sounds. Listen to these groups of words. Pay special attention to the sound of the letters in bold. In which word is the sound different?

1. s**ou**nd   **ou**r   **ou**ght   fl**ow**er
2. s**aw**   **ou**ght   gr**ou**nd   c**au**se
3. mu**s**eum   bu**s**y   beautiful   u**s**e
4. **aw**ful   **a**nimal   terrible   C**a**lifornia
5. person**a**l   person**a**lity   re**a**lity   It**a**lian
6. famou**s**   **s**ound   **c**ow   **s**hout
7. **sh**ip   wi**sh**   va**c**ation   **t**ime
8. famou**s**   fa**sc**inate   **c**ity   television
9. fa**sc**inate   fa**sc**inating   bu**s**iness   ho**l**iday

Now say the words aloud.

2. Stress and Intonation. First listen to the four questions below. Then read questions 1 and 2 aloud. Show with your voice that you already know what the answer will be.

1. It isn't my decision, **is it**? It's yours!
2. We won't be alive 200 years from now, **will we**?

Now read questions 3 and 4 aloud. This time show with your voice that you aren't sure of the answer—that you will be surprised if the answer is *Yes*.

3. That boy isn't really a thief, **is he**?
4. He won't be sent to prison, **will he**?

Listen to all the questions again. Did you sound the same way?

3. Complete these questions.

1. He didn't really steal that man's wallet, ...?
2. We all saw him do it, ...?
3. You already know this, ...?
4. This isn't so difficult, ...?
5. You've studied all this before, ...?
6. You'll remember all this, ...?
7. Sometimes it's difficult to think of the right word in English, ...?
8. I'm not boring you, ...?

After you have completed the eight questions above, try reading them aloud to someone else. Get the other person or people to tell you how you sounded. Was your question:

a. a *real* question—is it clear from your voice that you don't know the answer, and really want to hear it?
b. not a *real* question—is it clear from your voice that you already know the answer?

▶ UNIT 8

3 READING, THINKING, AND LISTENING

A. Reading

1. Read these three letters to an advice column. Each writer has a problem. Explain what it is.

1 A few months ago my girlfriend was offered a job in New York. I told her she shouldn't let our relationship stand in the way, but, to be honest, I never thought she would take it. Last week she told me she had decided to accept it. She'll be there for two years, and I think that's too long. Of course, we could travel back and forth to see each other, but that's not the point. She says if I really loved her, I'd wait for her. I think if she really loved me, she wouldn't want to be apart at all. What do you think? Is she right, or am I?

2 I've just moved to a new school in a different town. None of the other girls at the school are friendly, and I can't stand the boys. I never stop wishing that I was back at my old school, where I had lots of friends. What would you do if you were me?

3 My boyfriend is really getting on my nerves with his silly moods. All I have to do is look at another guy and he gets jealous. Last week we went to a party together and I danced with another boy — once! Afterwards, my boyfriend wouldn't talk to me for the rest of the night! He's making my life miserable and I think we should stop seeing each other. However, I don't know what he would do if I told him this. He's said several times that if I ever leave him, he'll kill himself. Sometimes I think he'd kill me, too, if I let him know how I really feel. What can I do about this awful problem?

2. Give your opinion. Do your classmates agree?

1. Which of these three people do you think probably feels:
   a. angry and upset?
   b. frightened?
   c. lonely and depressed?
2. Which of the writers do you think is probably the youngest of the three? Explain why you think so.
3. Which one do you think is probably the oldest? Tell why you think so.

3. This is the advice given to one of the three people. Which person? Why do you think so?

"Many men and women have been faced with the same situation before, especially in time of war or sometimes because of other circumstances, such as their jobs. If you really love each other, you will be able to find a way to overcome your problems."

What do you think the rest of the advice was? Try to guess!

4. Pretend the other two writers are friends of yours.

1. Which one would you find easier to give advice to? What would you advise this person to do?
2. Which writer would you find more difficult to give advice to? Can you think of anything to say that might help that person? Or is there something more you would like to know before giving advice? If so, what?

B. Listening

🎧 Listen to this conversation with the writer of one of the letters. Then answer these questions.

1. Which letter did one of the speakers write?
2. Why do you think so?
3. Who could the other speaker be?
4. As you listen, can you imagine what either of the speakers looks like? If so, try to describe him or her.
5. What does one of the speakers think is the cause of the other speaker's problems?
6. What does this speaker think the other one should do?

4 LANGUAGE STUDY

A. Giving Advice with *should (not)* and *ought (not) to*

1. Study this conversation.

A: This job is important to Jennifer. You should be more understanding.
B: I know I should, but . . .
A: Really! You shouldn't worry. Everything will turn out just fine.
B: Yes, I'm sure you're right. Thanks for the advice.

Can you say the conversation with *ought to* or *ought not to*?

2. Say these sentences a different way using the words in parentheses.

Example   If I were you, I wouldn't worry. (*shouldn't*)
              You shouldn't worry.

1. If I were you, I'd take the job in New York. (*should*)
2. If I were your boyfriend, I'd visit you there once in a while. (*ought to*)
3. If I were you, I'd go back to Los Angeles and visit him sometimes too. (*should*)
4. If I were you, I wouldn't let this job interfere with your relationship. (*shouldn't*)
5. If I were your boyfriend, I wouldn't be so selfish. (*shouldn't*)
6. If I were him, I'd appreciate your success. (*ought to*)

3. Match each situation or problem (1–8) with the appropriate advice (a–h).

1. A: I guess my son isn't very friendly. The other students don't seem to like him.
   B: ....
2. A: But it's 3,000 miles from Los Angeles to New York. I'll never see her if she takes that job.
   B: ....
3. A: Look. That guy across the room is looking at me. What should I do?
   B: ....
4. A: This exercise is too easy. I don't want to do it!
   B: ....
5. A: She has a terrible cold and she has a big test tomorrow.
   B: ....
6. A: I really don't know if I should continue to study English.
   B: ....
7. A: My girlfriend wants to go to a movie tonight, but I want to stay home.
   B: ....
8. A: My car broke down, so I left it on the highway.
   B: ....

a. If I were you, I'd go with her.
b. I'd go get it if I were you.
c. I think you should do it anyway.
d. Why don't you go to an early movie?
e. Maybe he should see a psychiatrist.
f. Well, if I were you, I wouldn't stop studying yet.
g. She probably ought to stay home and take the test another day.
h. I think you should ignore him.

B. Vocabulary Development

a. I'm very fond of you.
b. I'm crazy about you.
c. I envy you.
d. You're getting on my nerves.
e. I can't stand you.
f. Don't be such a fool.

1. Which of these sentences above (1–6) is closest in meaning to the sentences below (a–f)?

a. I like you, but I don't really love you.
b. You're doing something very silly.
c. I wish I were in your situation and had the things you have.
d. I can't stop thinking about you! I dream about you all the time.
e. I really hate you.
f. Stop doing that. It bothers me!

2. Which sentences don't make sense? Can you find any that do make sense? Change each sentence that doesn't make sense.

1. I'm terrified of friendly dogs.
2. Anna was so furious at her boyfriend that she felt like kissing him.
3. You don't know how much I miss you and how lonely I am without you.
4. What an awful movie! I was so fascinated that I walked out in the middle of it.
5. The book was so boring that I could hardly keep my eyes closed while I was reading it.
6. I really envy you! You're so unhappy and have nothing I've ever wanted!
7. My neighbor is always playing loud music, even late at night. It's really getting on my nerves!
8. Do you mind if I ask you a few very personal questions? I hope they will embarrass you.
9. We're all looking forward to seeing you again, and we'll be very disappointed if you come.
10. You should never be envious of someone else's bad luck.

3. On a personal level. Review the words in the box.

- astonished
- bored
- delighted
- depressed
- disappointed
- embarrassed
- fascinated
- furious
- terrified
- lonely

How would you feel if. . .

1. two strange men with knives walked toward you?
2. it rained and rained and you never saw the sun for days?
3. you wanted to see a movie, but when you got to the theater there were no more tickets?
4. someone poured red paint on your car just for a joke?
5. you said some bad things about someone who you didn't know was sitting behind you and could hear every word?
6. you had no friends—nobody to talk to—for a very long time?
7. you saw an elephant flying through the air?
8. you had to do the same stupid thing over and over again?
9. you could see real pictures of life on another planet?
10. you ran into an old friend you hadn't seen in several years?

4. Complete these sentences with the correct word.

1. John was fascinated .... Mary the moment he saw her.
2. At first, she wasn't interested .... him at all.
3. Then she noticed how sad he looked and began to feel sorry .... him.
4. "You look worried .... something. What is it?" she asked.
5. He told her he was .... love .... her.
6. When they started going out together, she found that he got jealous .... her very easily.
7. He used to get very angry .... her whenever she looked at another man.
8. She began to feel afraid .... him.

5 DISCUSSION AND WRITING

A. Reading

Here is another letter to an advice column. Read it carefully, ignoring the missing words. Then do the exercises.

I have an eighteen-year-old son who, like so many people his ¹............ these days, is finding it very difficult to get a job. In fact, I don't think he's even interested in trying to get ²............ anymore. But what worries me more than this is that he always seems to have ³............ money to go to discos and buy expensive clothes and things. When I ask him how he can possibly ⁴............ such things, he just smiles and says I wouldn't understand if he told me.

A few days ago, when I was cleaning his room, I found a leather wallet under his bed. I knew it wasn't his and when I ⁵............ inside, I found a credit card with someone else's name on it. I was absolutely horrified. I can't bear the thought that my own son may be a thief, but what other ⁶............ is there?

Since then, I've been so confused and upset that I can't even bring ⁷............ to talk to him about it. I just don't know ⁸............ to do. Do you think I ought to tell the police about it? Wouldn't it be terrible if I ⁹............? And yet, if I let him get away with it, isn't it possible that he'll just ¹⁰............ a professional criminal?

1. Give your opinion. Do your classmates agree?

1. Do you think the writer is a mother or a father? Why?
2. Why does it seem that the son is a thief?
3. How else could he be getting his money?
4. What would you do if you were the writer? Why?

2. Here are six of the missing words. Where do they belong? What are the other four missing words?

a. did   b. enough   c. myself
d. become   e. one   f. explanation

3. Discuss these questions.

1. What are some other problems that parents have with their children?
2. Do children ever have problems with their parents? If so, describe some of these problems.
3. What is some advice you can give for one of these problems?

4. On a personal level. Describe a difficult situation in which you needed advice. This can be something from your own experience or something imaginary.

Example "A friend of mine wanted to borrow some money. I didn't think he would pay it back, but I didn't want to hurt his feelings. I just didn't know what to do."

B. Writing

1. Based on the situation you described in Exercise 4 above, write a letter to an advice column. Try to write at least four sentences.
2. Give your letter to another classmate. The classmate will answer your letter, giving appropriate advice.

LANGUAGE SUMMARY FOR UNIT 7

1. Using the definite article when it's necessary

Do you like music?
Do you like the music they are playing?
I've always been interested in science and mathematics in general.
I've always been interested in the science of management, although some people prefer to call it an art.

2. Talking about how often things happen

He hardly ever attended classes.
He was constantly in trouble.
He occasionally did some experiments.
I read books about science now and then.
I seldom watch television.
I frequently listen to the radio.
She phones me once in a while.
I go jogging regularly.

3. Giving additional information with relative clauses

Einstein, who won the Nobel Prize for physics in 1921, was a brilliant man.
The Theory of Relativity, which concerns time and gravity and how things change when they travel at very high speeds, made him famous.
Most people don't understand the work which/that was done by Einstein.
I've never met anyone who/that is as important as Einstein.

4. Using the superlative

When he was a child in school, Einstein did not appear to be one of the brightest students.
However, today many people feel Einstein was the greatest scientist who ever lived.
It is certainly true that his Theory of Relativity is one of the most important concepts in science.

5. Using *always* and the progressive form to complain about someone

David is always talking about Einstein.
You're always criticizing me.
This machine is always breaking down.

6. Vocabulary Development

Suffixes -er, -or, *and* -ist:

murder: I'm not a murderer!
act: James Dean was a famous actor.
science: Einstein was a great scientist.

Words that describe intelligence:

intelligent: bright, brainy, sharp, smart, brilliant
unintelligent: slow, dumb, stupid, thick, dense

When he was a child, Einstein appeared to be slow, but he was actually a brilliant scientist.

7. Pronunciation

Stress and Intonation:
Does he get on your nerves sometimes?
  Yes, he does. Wouldn't he get on **yours**, too?

Words and Sounds:
1. thick   sick
2. change   champagne
3. check   chemistry
4. choose   shoes
5. watch   wash

LANGUAGE SUMMARY FOR UNIT 8

1. Talking about hypothetical situations in the present

What would you do if you saw someone steal someone else's wallet?
    If I saw someone stealing someone else's wallet, I'd try to stop him.
That could be dangerous. If I were you, I'd call the police.
    Yes. Maybe you're right. I wouldn't want to get hurt.

2. Giving advice

You should take the job in New York.
Your boyfriend ought to try to visit you there once in a while.
Your boyfriend shouldn't be so selfish.

3. Vocabulary Development

I'm very fond of you.
I'm crazy about you.
I envy you.
You're getting on my nerves.
I can't stand you.
Don't be such a fool.
She began to feel sorry for him.
You look worried about something.
He told her he was in love with her.
He got jealous of her very easily.
He used to get very angry at/with her.
She began to feel afraid of him.
I'd be astonished if I saw an elephant flying through the air.
I'd be delighted if she'd go out with me.
I'd be depressed if it rained and rained and I never saw the sun.
I'd be furious if someone poured red paint on my car.

4. Pronunciation

Words and Sounds:
1. s**ou**nd   fl**ow**er   **ou**ght
2. s**aw**   **ou**ght   c**au**se   gr**ou**nd
3. m**u**seum   b**eau**tiful   b**u**sy
4. awf**ul**   anim**al**   terribl**e**   Californi**a**
5. person**a**lity   person**a**l
6. s**ou**nd   c**ow**   fam**ou**s
7. wi**sh**   vaca**ti**on   **t**ime
8. famou**s**   fa**sc**inate   **c**ity   televi**s**ion
9. fa**sc**inate   bu**s**iness

Stress and Intonation:
There are two different ways to ask these questions:

a. a *real* question—it is clear from your voice that you don't know the answer, and really want to hear it.
That boy isn't really a thief, is he?
He won't be sent to prison, will he?
b. not a *real* question—it is clear from your voice that you already know the answer.
It isn't my decision, is it? It's yours!
We won't be alive 200 years from now, will we?

UNIT 9 News from the Future

1 READING AND THINKING

A. Reading

Read these brief news reports from the future. What is it in each article that tells you it is news from the future and not news of today?

the WORLD

PARALYZED MAN WALKS AGAIN

Two years ago, a young New York police officer, Luther Howard, was paralyzed in a car crash in which his back and spinal cord were broken. He was told he would never walk again. However, six months ago, he became a patient at the Columbia School of Bio-Medical Research. There, scientists were able to help him grow new nerve cells around the damaged area of his spine. Yesterday, he took his first steps since the accident.

SOVIET AND AMERICAN ASTRONAUTS LAND ON MARS

Two members of the joint Soviet–American mission to Mars, Yuri Rostropovich and Monica Valerio, became the first humans to walk on the surface of Mars yesterday. They will stay on the planet for three days before beginning the return journey to Earth. One of their objectives is to discover if there is any frozen water beneath the surface of the planet.

NEW anti-smoking campaign

Regina Salubre, European Minister of Health, has announced a new campaign against smoking in all EEC countries. Heavier fines for anyone who lights a cigarette, cigar, or pipe in a public place are planned, as well as compulsory treatment in local Anti-Nicotine Clinics. Mrs. Salubre also appealed to relatives or friends of "secret smokers" to inform the Public Health Police about them.

CURE FOR CANCER FOUND

A team of French scientists at the Institut Pasteur have announced the discovery of a new superdrug to cure cancer. Dr. Gilbert Dalgaglian, head of the team, claims that tests with human beings have been "remarkably successful and have shown no serious side-effects." He said he believed that it would cure 90% of all but a few rare types of cancer.

UNIT 9

Monday, June 21, 2015

Are people living too long?

Yesterday at an international conference in Montreal on population trends, experts discussed new techniques of biological engineering that will soon increase average life expectancy to 150 years. However, they were warned that this will add to the problems that have already been caused by the tendency to live longer.

Only a few years ago, in Canada and other parts of the world, people were regarded as "old" when they reached the age of 60 or 70, and rarely lived beyond 80 or 90. Now, however, with more and more people living to be 120 or more, it is becoming increasingly difficult to pay for the pensions and care that they regard as their natural rights.

What is more, many older people are now demanding the right to continue working until they are 90, or even older, rather than being forced to retire at 60 or 65. This means that many younger people find that their chances of promotion are blocked because older colleagues above them are holding on to their jobs instead of giving them up.

B. Matching

The last sentence of each article is missing. Can you find it below?

1. As a result, the disease would soon be mainly a subject for the history books.
2. If there is, a second mission will be sent there next year for the purpose of building a research station in which scientists from both countries will be able to spend up to six months.
3. Doctors say that within a year he will be able to walk and run again and even to play his favorite sport, basketball.
4. This could easily lead to an explosive situation in society unless something is done about it very soon.
5. She added that unless this unhealthy habit is stamped out once and for all, the authorities will be forced to take even more extreme measures.

C. True or False?

According to the text, which of these statements are true? Which are false? If there isn't enough information in the text, say "It doesn't say."

1. The police officer's injury was not very serious.
2. He is making excellent progress now.
3. The Soviet-American astronauts think there may be some water somewhere on Mars.
4. The Russians and Americans have already decided to send a mission to Mars after this one.
5. The new French drug will be used to stop people from smoking.
6. The new French drug will cure most but not all types of serious diseases.
7. International experts are worried because not enough people are living to 120 or more.
8. As people grow older, many of them want to go on working longer.

D. Discussion

Give your opinion. Do your classmates agree?

1. Which of the things in the news reports do you hope will be possible someday? Why?
2. Is there anything in any of the articles that is already possible today?
3. Is there anything that you think will never be possible? What? Why not?
4. Is there anything that you hope will never happen? What? Why not?

▶ UNIT 9

2 LANGUAGE STUDY

A. Can and be able to

1. Study these sentences.

1. The average person is able to live quite a long time now.
2. Were you able to do yesterday's homework assignment?
3. I don't know if I'll be able to go with you tomorrow.
4. We'd be able to live much longer if scientists found a way to prevent the body from aging.

Say the sentences above with *can* or *could* instead of *be able to*. Refer to the chart below.

Tense	Can	Be able to
Present:	can	is/am/are able to
Past:	could	was/were able to
Future:	can	will be able to
Conditional:	could	would be able to

2. Study the words in *italics*. Do they mean *was/were (not) able to* or *would (not) be able to*? How do you know?

1. She *couldn't* fix her car herself. She had to take it to a mechanic.
2. I know it's difficult, but you *could* do it if you tried.
3. They *couldn't* do the exercise if the teacher didn't explain it.
4. *Could* he do the exercise, or didn't he understand it?

3. Complete the sentences with *be able to*.

Example   The doctor tried everything, but she .... not .... help me.
The doctor tried everything, but she wasn't able to help me.

1. I .... read and write English much better now than I used to.
2. .... doctors .... cure most cases of cancer? Or are there still many types of cancer they don't know anything about?
3. We can do a lot of things as adults that we .... not .... do as children.
4. I .... not .... save any money if I went out all the time—you know, to movies and restaurants and places like that.
5. I don't know if I .... help you. I'll call you later and tell you.

6. A: I didn't pass my English test.
   B: Well, if you studied a little harder, you .... pass all your tests.

4. On a personal level. Continue this conversation with a classmate and talk about yourself.

A: I can do a lot of things as an adult that I wasn't able to do as a child.
B: What are you able to do now that you couldn't do then?

B. Can vs. will be able to

1. Study these examples. It is necessary to use *will be able to* rather than *can* in two of them. Why?

1. My eyesight is very poor right now, but the doctors tell me that after the operation I'll be able to see almost perfectly.
2. I'm pretty busy today, but maybe I can see you tomorrow.
3. This article says that someday soon we'll be able to cure almost all major diseases.
4. He's young and healthy. I'm sure he can find a job.

Which two are examples of:

a. something that hasn't happened but which the person can already do?
b. an ability purely in the future—something that needs something else to happen first, such as a new discovery?

2. In which of these sentences is it possible to use *can*? In which is it necessary to use *will be able to*? Explain why.

1. He lost a leg in the accident. But with a new artificial one, he .... walk again.
2. After a few more lessons, I think you .... ski very well.
3. I don't really feel like going to the movies tonight. .... we go tomorrow instead?
4. If we meet in town tomorrow, we .... have lunch in that new restaurant.
5. Do you think that someday people .... live and work on other planets?
6. I'm hard-of-hearing, but if I get a hearing aid I .... hear everything people say.

C. Unless vs. if

1. Which two sentences are the same in meaning? Which two are very different?

1. Unless you have this operation, you will die.
2. If you have this operation, you will die.
3. Unless I study, I'll fail the exam.
4. If I don't study, I'll fail the exam.

Look again at the two sentences that are different. Can you change one of the sentences so they are the same in meaning?

2. Study the beginning of these sentences (1–6). Find the best way to end each one (a–f).

1. Unless I earn some more money,
2. If I earn some more money,
3. Unless I get to the station in twenty minutes,
4. If I get to the station in twenty minutes,
5. Unless you give me that money,
6. If you give me the money,

a. I'll miss the train.
b. I'll be able to buy a new car.
c. I'll shoot you.
d. I won't be able to buy a new car.
e. nothing will happen to you.
f. I'll just be able to catch the train.

3. Complete this conversation with *if* or *unless*.

A: You will only get sicker [1] .... you don't go to the doctor.
B: I never go to the doctor [2] .... I have something serious, and I only have an allergy.
A: [3] .... I'm not mistaken, an allergy can be very serious.
B: [4] .... I'm not better by tomorrow, I promise to go see the doctor.
A: Good. [5] .... you need a ride, I'll take you there myself.
B: Thanks. But I'll walk [6] .... it rains.

D. Pronunciation: Words and Sounds

1. 📼 Listen to these words. Pay special attention to the sound of the *t* and how it changes. Then practice pronouncing the words.

| operate | operation | direct | direction |
| promote | promotion | inspect | inspection |

In pairs or groups, practice pronouncing these words. What happens to the sound of the *t*?

complete	completion
invent	invention
elect	election
fascinate	fascination
congratulate	congratulations
associate	association

2. Complete these sentences with the correct form of the word in parentheses. How is the word pronounced?

1. (*pronounce*) How can I improve my ....?
2. (*describe*) Here's a .... of the criminal.
3. (*intend*) I have no .... of doing that.
4. (*explain*) Listen to this ....
5. (*introduce*) He gave me a letter of ....
6. (*depress*) Do you ever suffer from ....?
7. (*fascinate*) I don't understand your .... with him.
8. (*invent*) Isn't television an incredible ....?

▶ UNIT 9

3 READING AND DISCUSSION

Average Life Expectancy in Europe and North America

| Roman Times | Middle Ages | Mid 19th Century | End 19th Century | 1920's | 1940's | 1960's | 1980's | 2000's | 2090's | 2100's |

A. Reading

1. Study the graph above and answer these questions.

1. Part of the graph is based on actual facts and statistics. Which part?
2. What do you think the other parts are based on?

2. Explain what the graph says.

1. Make sentences like this about other periods up to the 1980s:
   The average life expectancy of a person living in Roman times was 25 years.
2. Make sentences like this for other periods after 2000:
   If the experts are right, many people around the year 2000 will be living until they . . . (what is the rest of the sentence?)
3. Using information from the graph, compare different periods like this:
   Between Roman times and the Middle Ages, life expectancy rose from 25 to 35 years.
4. How many sentences can you make like this?:
   According to this graph, life expectancy will rise from . . . to . . . between . . . and . . . .

B. Discussion

Discuss these questions.

1. What other changes besides changes in life expectancy occurred in some of the periods on the graph?
2. Choose at least one of these periods and talk about your own country. Describe such things as:
   a. the changes in the way people lived.
   b. anything else you know about the period, such as wars, new inventions, or other changes.
3. Here are some words used to describe people in different periods of their life:
   - an infant • a child • an adolescent
   - a teenager • a young adult • middle-aged
   - a senior citizen • elderly • very old

   How old is a person in each of these periods? Find out if other people in your class agree with you.
4. Here is a description of what happens to some people in one of these periods of life:

   Around this time of life, a lot of people begin to get fat. Men start to go bald and women start to worry about wrinkles. But very often people at this age begin to earn a lot of money.

   Which period do you think is being described? Why? What other changes sometimes happen to people at this time of life?
5. Describe another period in life, but don't say which it is. See if people in your class can guess which period you are talking about.

4 LANGUAGE STUDY

A. The Conditional in Possible *What will happen if . . .?* and Hypothetical *What would happen if . . .?* Situations

1. Study these situations. Which one suggests the speaker has a good chance of going to medical school?

1. I'll specialize in medical care for the elderly if I go to medical school.
2. I'd specialize in medical care of the elderly if I went to medical school.

Can you explain what the speakers mean in the two sentences below?

3. I'll take you to a movie tonight if I have time.
4. I'd take you to a movie tonight if I had time.

2. There is only one way to complete each of these sentences. Is it a, b, or c?

1. What .... happen in the future if people live until they are 120 or even longer?
   a. would   b. does   c. will

2. Will you be happy if you .... that long?
   a. live   b. will live   c. would live

3. There will be lots of problems if the average life expectancy .... to increase.
   a. would continue   b. continues   c. continued

4. Do you know that your chances of living longer .... better if you stopped smoking and drinking?
   a. would be   b. were   c. will be

5. Would you be surprised if I .... you that someday people may live until they are 150 or even older?
   a. tell   b. would tell   c. told

6. Of course, this .... possible only if we continue our research into the causes of aging.
   a. would be   b. will be   c. were

7. Unless we .... this, no progress will be made.
   a. don't do   b. won't do   c. do

8. Do you have any idea what you will be doing when you .... 65?
   a. will be   b. are   c. would be

3. On a personal level. Interview a classmate. Use the conversation below.

A: What do you think will happen if people start living until they are 120 or even older?
B: ....
A: Would you be happy if you lived that long?
B: ....
A: Some experts feel that there will be a lot of problems if people live longer. What do you think?
B: ....
A: Can you suggest any solutions to these possible problems?
B: ....

B. The Simple Future (*will do*) vs. the Future Progressive (*will be doing*)

1. Study these sentences.

1. What will you do at 7:00 tomorrow morning?
2. What will you be doing at 7:00 tomorrow morning?
3. I'll be having breakfast at 7:00.
4. I'll have breakfast at 7:00.

Which situation below (a–d) does each of the sentences above (1–4) go best with?

a. You want to find out if someone will already be up and out of bed around seven o'clock tomorrow morning.
b. Someone has just asked you if you will be up and out of bed at seven o'clock. You want to say that you will be in the middle of breakfast at that time.
c. You are in a hotel. You are telling the receptionist when you want breakfast tomorrow morning.
d. You are the head of a gang of criminals. Tomorrow the gang will rob a bank. Each person has to follow a step-by-step plan from seven o'clock onwards. You are asking questions about the plan to make sure everyone understands it exactly.

2. Complete the sentences with the Future Progressive (*she'll be working*). Use the verbs in parentheses.

Example A: When .... she .... for New York? (*leave*)
B: She .... for a month. (*not leave*)

A: *When will she be leaving for New York?*
B: *She won't be leaving for a month.*

A: Have you seen Jennifer lately?
B: Yes, I saw her yesterday. She said she ¹............ to New York soon. (*move*)
A: Oh, that's right. I forgot. Do you know what she ²............ there? (*do*)
B: She ³............ for an advertising company. (*work*)
A: ⁴............ she .... a lot more money? (*make*)
B: Oh, I'm sure she will be.
A: And how does she feel about the move?
B: She's excited. She said she ⁵............ a very different life in New York. (*lead*)
A: ⁶............ Tony .... with her? (*go*)
B: No. He ⁷............ (*not go*)

3. What is the best response to each sentence?

1. I'll call you around 10:00.
   a. Please don't. I'll be sleeping.
   b. Please don't. I'll sleep.

2. The plane trip from Los Angeles to New York is about five hours. What will you do?
   a. I'll be sleeping.
   b. I'll sleep.

3. Will she be able to study at home if her brother is having a party tonight?
   a. No. She'll be studying at the library.
   b. No. She'll study at the library.

4. Do you think she'll be at home between 3:00 and 4:00?
   a. No. She'll be studying at the library.
   b. No. She'll study at the library.

5. Maybe I'll stop and see you at your store on Saturday.
   a. I won't be working that day.
   b. I won't work that day.

6. What will you do about your job if your sister decides to get married on a Saturday?
   a. I won't be working that day.
   b. I won't work that day.

4. On a personal level. Talk about yourself and find out about your classmates.

1. Look at your watch. What is the exact time? Say what you will be doing at this same exact time tomorrow.
2. What time do you think you will probably do these things tomorrow?
   a. get up   c. have dinner
   b. have lunch   d. go to bed
3. Think of other things that you usually do at certain times of the day or on certain days of the week. Then say when you will do these things tomorrow or next week.
4. What question should you ask someone else if you want to get the same information from that person that you have just given about yourself?
5. Find out what other people in your class will be doing at the times below. If they aren't sure, ask them to tell you what they will probably be doing or what they hope they will be doing.
   a. 10 A.M. next Monday
   b. 5 P.M. tomorrow evening
   c. 9 P.M. the day after tomorrow
   d. 1 P.M. next Saturday

C. Pronunciation: Words and Sounds

▶ Listen to these words. How does the sound of the letter in bold change? What else changes?

1. **a**ble   **a**bility
2. **e**xplain   **e**xplanation
3. **a**llergy   **a**llergic
4. fr**a**gile   fr**a**gility

Now say the words aloud.

5 READING, LISTENING, AND WRITING

A. Reading

Two young people tell an interviewer what they hope they will be doing ten years from now. Read the interviews and then answer the questions.

"I'll have a good car. That's really important . . . to have a really good car. I'll have all the money I need. And I'll be famous. I'll be able to travel all over the world. When I go into a restaurant, people will turn and look at me and say, 'Oh, look! There's that famous racecar driver!'

"I won't have to get up early every morning. I'll be able to stay out late at night and go to lots of parties and things like that.

"Maybe I'll be married by then and have a nice family. Or maybe I'll have lots of girlfriends instead. I'll have a house with a big swimming pool in California and four cars in the garage. And I'll have another big house somewhere else, where I can go for the winter—Switzerland or France, so I can ski. Or the Caribbean."

"I'll still be working, but things will be different. With any luck, I'll be earning more money, but the most important thing will be the job itself and how interesting it is. Of course, I'd like to have more money and more authority than I do now, but I don't think that's the only thing in life. What I really want is . . . is to be more independent than I am now . . . to have more control over my own life.

"Then someday I'd like to do something entirely different . . . maybe open a small restaurant or write a book or something like that. I'm not really sure if I'll ever have children . . . or even if I'll get married. It all depends if I meet the right person. But I won't feel that my life is empty and meaningless if I'm still living alone ten years . . . or even twenty years from now. Not at all! My mother is always saying, 'There's nothing like a good relationship!' But I'm not so sure. There's nothing worse than a bad one either!"

Questions

1. Which of these people do you think is probably older and more experienced than the other? Why?
2. Is there anything they say they hope for or want that you also want or hope for?
3. Is there anything they say they want or hope for that you don't think is very important?

B. Listening

Listen to what the mother of a young man hopes her son will be doing ten years from now.

1. What do you think the speaker means when she says, "I hope he'll have settled down by then"? What do people do when they "settle down"?
2. What kind of job does she think would be good for her son? Why?
3. What kind of job does she think wouldn't be right for him? Why not?
4. What is the "huge responsibility" she talks about?

C. Writing

1. In pairs or groups, talk about these things.

1. Imagine a day in your life ten years from now. What do you hope it will be like?
2. Where will you be living? In a big/small house or an apartment? Describe this place.
3. Will you have a job? If you hope you won't have to work, what will you do with your time?
4. If you are not already married, what about marriage and children? If you are married and have children, do you have any hopes for them?

2. Write two or three paragraphs describing "A day in my life ten years from now." Be sure to:

1. think about what you said while discussing the questions in Exercise 1.
2. write about what you hope this day will be like.

UNIT 10 A Threatened Planet

1 READING, THINKING, AND LISTENING

A. Pre-reading

Look at the pictures. Then answer these questions.

1. What do you know about the animal in the top picture?
2. When did it live and why did it die?
3. Look at the smaller picture. What can you see?
4. Why are scientists so interested in these different layers of rock and clay?

B. Reading

Read the text and then answer the questions below.

The strange light appeared in the sky very suddenly. At first, perhaps for a second, it was very small, like a match being lit in the night. But then it quickly became extremely bright—a hundred times brighter than the sun. Then, just as suddenly, the sea "exploded." There is no other way to describe it.

The roar of the explosion was so loud that it could have been heard on the other side of the world. There were, however, no humans on earth at that time to hear it. It happened 65 million years ago. The light was a very large and very heavy meteor which probably weighed billions of tons. When it broke through the earth's atmosphere and crashed into the sea, the water was changed into a kind of gas and the meteor was like a barrel of fire. How do we know this explosion really happened? And what could have caused it? To answer these two questions, we must first consider another mystery.

About two hundred years ago, the first fossils, or bones, of a huge prehistoric animal were found. Scientists studied the bones and discovered that it was a kind of reptile. They called this reptile a "dinosaur." They also discovered that these giant animals lived on the earth for millions of years but then, suddenly, and perhaps as the result of a catastrophe, disappeared.

Below the ground there are many different layers of rock and clay. Each period of the earth's history has a particular layer. The bones of dinosaurs are found in one layer. Then there is a thin layer of clay. In the next layer after this, we find the bones of different kinds of animals, but no more dinosaurs.

There is something very strange about the thin layer of clay between the bones of the dinosaurs and the bones of the animals that came after them. This thin layer of clay is very rich in two very unusual metals called osmium and iridium. Certain types of meteors contain large amounts of iridium and osmium. The concentrations of these metals in that thin layer of clay might have come from such a meteor—the largest and heaviest that has ever hit the earth. It could have had the energy of 5 billion (5,000 million) atomic bombs of the size that was dropped on Nagasaki in August 1945.

This explosion could have caused a long period of darkness. The sun rose and set each day as before, but its rays were unable to penetrate through the cloud of gas that covered the earth. This period of darkness might have lasted as long as 5 years. Millions of animals would have died and, for various reasons, large animals that lived on the land would have suffered the most. The dinosaur was just one of the animals that disappeared in perhaps the greatest catastrophe that has ever taken place on this earth.

Questions

1. What was the "strange light" in the sky 65 million years ago?
2. Explain why the sea suddenly "exploded."
3. What exactly is meant by the phrase "a long period of darkness"?
4. Explain how the thin layer of clay has helped us to understand what happened.
5. How do we know that dinosaurs existed 65 million years ago and then, suddenly, disappeared?
6. Describe what might have happened after the meteor hit the earth.

C. Listening

Listen to this part of a popular science program that was broadcast on the radio recently. Then answer the questions.

1. Explain what a "sudden change" could mean in geology.
2. What does the scientist mean when she says she "accepts" the theory that a huge meteor struck the earth 65 million years ago?
3. How often, according to one theory, do very large meteors strike the earth?
4. The scientist mentions another theory about how often they strike. Which theory would you prefer to believe is true? Why?

▶ UNIT 10

2 LANGUAGE STUDY

A. Might (may) vs. could vs. should (ought to)

1. Study these sentences.

1. I might (may) listen to the science program on the radio tonight.
2. I could listen to the science program on the radio tonight.
3. I should (ought to) listen to the science program on the radio tonight.

Which sentence above is similar in meaning to:

a. It would be a good idea if I listened to the science program because we are studying dinosaurs in school.
b. I'm thinking about listening to the science program, but I'm not 100% sure I will.
c. I'd be able to listen to the science program tonight—if I wanted to.

2. Complete this conversation with *might (may)*, *could*, or *should (ought to)*.

A: We ¹............ go to that new science fiction movie this afternoon. Would you like to join us?
B: When will you decide if you're going?
A: Well, we ²............ decide soon because I invited Bill and I have to let him know.
B: Well, to tell you the truth, I'm a little tired today, but I ³............ go with you tomorrow afternoon if you wanted to wait.
A: I think we ⁴............ go to the Museum of Natural History tomorrow afternoon. Or maybe we'll go tomorrow morning. We're not sure yet.
B: Oh, you'll enjoy that. I went yesterday. But you ⁵............ definitely go in the morning. There'll be fewer people. There's an exhibit on meteors, and it ⁶............ be very crowded if you go too late.
A: You're probably right.
B: In fact, you ⁷............ not get in at all if you wait until the afternoon.
A: Are you sure you don't want to go again? We ⁸............ get something to eat afterwards—I mean, if you didn't have anything else to do.
B: No, I don't think so.

B. Past Modals: *might (may) have done* and *could have done*

1. Study these pairs of sentences.

1. The darkness lasted for five years.
2. The darkness might have lasted for five years.

3. The metal in the clay came from a meteor.
4. The metal in the clay could have come from a meteor.

Which two sentences show that the speaker has no doubt that the sentences are true? What do the other two sentences show?

2. *Might have done*, *may have done*, and *could have done* often mean the same thing. Complete these sentences with the past form of the words in parentheses.

Example Sixty-five million years ago, there (*might be*) a tremendous explosion.
Sixty-five million years ago, there might have been a tremendous explosion.

1. According to one popular theory, a meteor (*may cause*) this explosion when it exploded in the earth's atmosphere.
2. This catastrophe (*might change*) the earth's climate.
3. It (*could cause*) the death of the dinosaurs.
4. Of course, there (*may be*) a different kind of catastrophe.
5. An explosion (*might not kill*) the dinosaurs.
6. It was a very long time ago and a number of things (*could have*) an effect on the earth's climate and its animals.

3. These are the fossil remains of a bird that died 65 million years ago. Change the explanations of why it died so that there is some doubt about them. Use *might (may)*, or *could*.

Example It died in the explosion.
It might have died in the explosion.

1. It died of a strange disease.
2. Another animal killed it.
3. The climate changed suddenly.
4. It didn't have any food.
5. Other animals ate its food.
6. It died simply of old age.

4. You have a friend named Bill. Bill is forgetful and confused at times. Think of a possible explanation for each situation. (There is usually more than one possible explanation.)

Example Bill can't find his glasses.
He might have lost them. **or**
He might have put them in another jacket.

1. You were expecting Bill to meet you at 3:00 in a coffee shop. It's already 3:15 and he still hasn't come.
2. When he finally arrives (at 3:30), he can't find his wallet.
3. He says he had it when he came into the restaurant. A man bumped into him as he came in.
4. When he gets home that evening, he finds his door open.
5. The next morning, his car isn't in front of his house. He can't remember if he walked home last night or not.

5. On a personal level. Imagine you have encountered the situations below. Your partner will offer an explanation for each one. Accept or reject the explanation.

Example A: I can't find my wallet.
  B: *You might have left it at home.*
  A: *No, I don't think so.* (or *You're probably right.*)

1. Have you seen my briefcase?
2. I put my homework on the desk, but it isn't there now.
3. My English teacher was late for class today.
4. I went over to ....'s house last night, but he/she wasn't home.
5. That's strange. I always have my car keys in my pocket, but they aren't there now.

C. Pronunciation: Words, Sounds, and Stress

1. 🔊 Listen to these sets of words. The second word in each set has *-ic* in it. How does the stress change?

1. history (his-to-ry)   historic (his-**tor**-ic)
2. atom (at-om)   atomic (a-**tom**-ic)
3. geography (ge-og-ra-phy)   geographic (ge-o-**graph**-ic)
4. metal (me-tal)   metallic (me-**tall**-ic)

2. Say these words aloud. Which syllable do you think should be stressed? Does the pronunciation sometimes change in other ways, too, when the stress changes?

1. phi-los-o-phy   phi-lo-soph-ic
2. ca-tas-tro-phe   ca-ta-stroph-ic
3. at-mo-sphere   at-mo-spher-ic
4. a-nal-y-sis   an-a-lyt-ic
5. e-con-o-my   ec-o-nom-ic
6. me-te-or   me-te-or-ic
7. pe-ri-od   pe-ri-od-ic
8. id-i-ot   id-i-ot-ic

🔊 Now listen to the words and check your pronunciation.

D. Vocabulary Development

Complete these sentences with the correct form of the word in *italics*. Use your dictionary if necessary.

1. (*explode*) Millions of animals probably died in the ....
2. (*destroy*) It caused a great deal of ....
3. (*concentrate*) How do you explain the .... of these metals?
4. (*suffer*) The famine has caused tremendous ....
5. (*disappear*) The sudden .... of the dinosaurs is a great mystery.
6. (*discover*) The .... of these fossils caused a big sensation.
7. (*describe*) The police have given the following .... of the criminal.
8. (*add*) In .... to the fossils of the dinosaurs, the bones of other animals were found.

▶ UNIT 10

3 READING AND LISTENING

▲ A. Reading

Children in different parts of the world recently wrote compositions about animals that are still alive but which are in danger of disappearing.

Read through the compositions, ignoring the missing words. What animals do you think the children were writing about?

Once, there were very large numbers of them in India and parts of Africa. But now they are almost extinct because people have been ¹_____ them for a long time. It is the fastest animal on land, but it's very timid and shy by nature. Lions do not like them because they hunt for the same kind of animals for food. But they can defend themselves against lions because they are so fast. There is only one animal they cannot defend themselves ²_____ . Us! Future generations may see them only in photographs unless we do something to save them NOW!

They look something like dogs, but they ³_____ in the sea. They are very playful and friendly. They are disappearing for two main reasons: hunting and pollution. I have seen terrible pictures of men killing the very young ones by hitting them over the heads with clubs. Thousands of them die every year so that rich women can walk around in fur ⁴_____ made from their skins. I hate women like that!

Not many people know that they ⁵_____ strange and beautiful songs in order to communicate with each other! These songs travel hundreds of miles through the sea. They are the biggest animals left on earth, and besides us, the most intelligent. Cruel men in dirty ships hunt them and kill them by shooting harpoons with explosives into their bodies. Soon, they will all be dead unless these men are stopped. There is nothing we get from them that we cannot make ⁶_____ . I think the worst thing of all is that some people actually eat meat from them or feed it to their pets.

Read the compositions again. Where do the three missing words below belong? What are the other three missing words?

a. sing   b. hunting   c. ourselves

▲ B. Listening

1. 📼 Listen to this short description of another animal. Then answer the questions.

1. How many legs does it have?
2. What are some of its other characteristics?
3. Who doesn't like this animal?
4. What else did you learn about it?
5. Can you guess what animal it is?
6. What common animal is it related to?

2. On a personal level. Work in groups of three or four. One of you must think of an animal. Don't give the name of this animal. Instead, give a short description of the animal like the ones in the compositions above. See if the other people in your group can guess what animal you are talking about.

4 LANGUAGE STUDY

A. Vocabulary Development: Reason, Cause, and Purpose

1. Study these definitions and notice how the words are used.

reason: the explanation or excuse for an action or event
The *reason* lions are hostile to cheetahs is that they both hunt the same animals.
What's the *reason* for your visit?

cause: a person, thing, or event that makes something happen
The *cause* of the fire was never discovered.
Careless driving is the *cause* of many terrible accidents.

purpose: intention or plan; reason for an action
What's the *purpose* of your visit?
The *purpose* of all this is to show you how three words can be similar in meaning but different in the way they are used.

2. Use *reason, cause,* and *purpose* to complete these sentences.

1. What was the ………… of the catastrophe?
2. The ………… I couldn't come to your party was that I was sick.
3. What is the ………… of this exercise?
4. What was the ………… for your strange behavior yesterday?
5. Accidents have many …………, but carelessness is one of the most common.
6. The ………… we're doing all these exercises is to improve your English.
7. The ………… of all these exercises is to improve your English.
8. Why did the dinosaurs suddenly die? I mean, what was the ………… of it?
9. Why are you trying to save so much money? I mean, what's the ………… of it?
10. There seems to be no ………… for killing whales. There is nothing we get from them that we cannot make from other things.

B. Expressing Purpose with *for, (in order) to,* and *so (that)*

1. Which part of each of these sentences shows the purpose of the action?

1. Men hunt them for money.
2. We must do something to protect them.
3. Men go out in dirty ships in order to kill them.
4. Thousands of these animals die so that a few people can walk around in fur coats.
5. We must do something soon so these animals won't become extinct.

Look again at the sentences above. What type of word follows *for*? What type of word follows *(in order) to*? *So (that)* is a bit different—what is it followed by?

2. Complete these sentences with *for, in order to,* and *so that*.

Examples In East Africa, tigers, elephants, zebras, and other wild animals have been hunted *for* sport as well as *for* economic reasons.

We must protect these animals *in order to* keep them from becoming extinct.

We must protect them *so that* future generations will be able to see more than just pictures of them.

1. Many of the elephants of East Africa have been killed ………… their ivory tusks.
2. For centuries, many other countries have imported ivory ………… make jewelry and other expensive items from ivory.
3. Some countries also imported ivory ………… they could make elegant knife, fork, and spoon handles and chopsticks.
4. The unfortunate zebra has been killed ………… people can use their skins for shoes, pocketbooks, and rugs.
5. ………… make fur coats, people have killed thousands of leopards over the years.
6. Recently, the countries in East Africa have passed laws ………… save these precious animals.
7. ………… they won't become extinct, these animals are being protected in special areas where hunting is not allowed.
8. Hopefully, people will begin to find substitutes ………… the things these wild animals supply.

To and *so* are a little less formal than *in order to* and *so that*. Say sentences 2–7 again, using only *to* and *so*.

3. Combine these sentences. Four of them can be combined with either *to* or *so*. The other four can only be combined with *so*. Which four?

Example I want to drive into town. Then I can buy some food.
I want to drive into town to buy some food.
I want to drive into town so I can buy some food.

1. I'm leaving for the station now. Then I can catch an earlier train.
2. I'll take you to the station now. Then you can catch an earlier train.
3. I have to earn more money. Then I can buy all the things I want.
4. I have to earn more money. Then you can buy all the things you want.
5. We put wild animals in cages. Then they can't escape.
6. Let's go on a safari. Then we can see all the wild animals.
7. Listen carefully. Then you can get the general meaning.
8. Speak more slowly, please. Then I can understand you.

4. First read this conversation. Then choose the best short answer (a–h) for each of speaker A's questions.

A: Why did your father go to Africa?
B: ¹............
A: To hunt wild animals?
B: ²............
A: Really? Why?
B: ³............
A: Why didn't you go with him?
B: ⁴............
A: Safaris are so hot and dusty. Why would you want to go, anyway?
B: ⁵............
A: Why do you think they will become extinct?
B: ⁶............
A: Why do they shoot them if there aren't very many of them?
B: ⁷............
A: Is that the only reason?
B: ⁸............
A: Oh, that's terrible!

a. Because people shoot them.
b. To go on a safari.
c. For money.
d. No. To photograph wild animals.
e. Because he's doing an assignment for a wildlife magazine.
f. No. To have fun too!
g. Because I couldn't take any time off.
h. So I could see those incredible animals before they become extinct.

5. On a personal level. Work in a group and discuss these questions.

1. What are some of the wild animals that are found in your country? What are some of the domestic animals that are found there?
2. Do you think it is important to protect certain kinds of animals? If so, what kinds and why?
3. Are there any animals that you think do not need protection? Why do you think so?
4. Do you think the world could exist with no animals at all? Why or why not?

5 WRITING

A. Matching

A fifteen-year-old girl wrote this. Read the first part of each sentence (1–9). Then find the next part (a–i).

New York Obituary

1. Early this morning, New York City suffocated
2. The city could not
3. It was rushed to the hospital, but
4. The disease (overpopulation and pollution) was discovered many years ago, and the city had shown many symptoms,
5. New York City contained
6. Many people loved
7. Its death will cause
8. Services will be

a. such as dead trees and grass, smog, backed-up sewers, and difficulty breathing.
b. a great deal of sorrow.
c. from pollution and harmful gases.
d. the city and its sights.
e. held on May 4th in the remains of Central Park.
f. it died on the way (the ambulance was caught in a traffic jam).
g. many people and important businesses.
h. breathe.

B. Writing

Think of a city or town you know that has some of the same problems as New York.

1. First, describe some of these problems.
2. Then suggest what you think could or should be done to solve some of these problems.
3. Finally, describe what you think may or will happen unless these problems are solved.

LANGUAGE SUMMARY FOR UNIT 9

1. Talking about present and past ability with *can* and *be able to*

I can do a lot of things as an adult that I wasn't able to do as a child.
　What are you able to do now that you couldn't do then?
I can stay out late at night for one thing. I could move to my own apartment, too, if I could afford it.

If you studied a little harder, you'd be able to pass all your tests.

2. Talking about future ability with *can* and *will be able to*

I'm pretty busy today, but maybe I can see you tomorrow.
This article says that someday soon we'll be able to cure almost all major diseases.

3. Using *unless* and *if*

Unless I study, I'll fail the exam.
If I don't study, I'll fail the exam.

4. Talking about possible situations (*What will happen if . . .?*) and hypothetical situations (*What would happen if . . .?*)

What do you think will happen if people start living until they are 120 or even older?
　Well, I think the earth will be very crowded if no one dies until they are that old.
Would you be happy if you lived that long?
　I guess I would if I were healthy and had enough money.

5. Using the Simple Future (*will do*) and the Future Progressive (*will be doing*)

What time will you get up tomorrow morning?
　I'll probably get up at 6:30.
What will you be doing at 7:00 tomorrow morning?
　I'll be having breakfast.

6. Pronunciation: Words, Sounds, and Stress

operate—operation
allergy—allergic
explain—explanation
able—ability

LANGUAGE SUMMARY FOR UNIT 10

1. Using *might (may), could*, and *should (ought to)*

We might go to that new science fiction movie this afternoon. Would you like to join us?
   I could go with you tomorrow afternoon if you wanted to wait.
We may go the Natural History Museum tomorrow afternoon.
   You should definitely go in the morning. There'll be fewer people.

2. Talking about possibility in the past (Past Modals)

You might/may have left your homework at home.
The metal in the clay could have come from a meteor.

3. Expressing purpose with *for*, *(in order) to*, and *so (that)*

Men hunt whales for money.
We must do something to protect them.
Men go out in dirty ships in order to kill them.
Thousands of these animals die so that a few people can walk around in fur coats.
We must do something soon so these animals won't become extinct.

4. Vocabulary Development

Verbs and Their Noun Forms:
1. explode—explosion
2. destroy—destruction
3. concentrate—concentration
4. suffer—suffering
5. disappear—disappearance
6. discover—discovery
7. describe—description
8. add—addition

Reason, Cause, and Purpose:
The reason lions are hostile to cheetahs is that they both hunt the same animals.
The cause of the fire was never discovered.
The purpose of all this is to show you how three words can be similar in meaning but different in the way they are used.

5. Pronunciation: Words, Sounds, and Stress

1. **his**tory   his**tor**ic
2. **at**om   a**tom**ic
3. ge**o**graphy   geo**graph**ic
4. **me**tal   me**tall**ic
5. phi**los**ophy   philo**soph**ic
6. ca**tas**trophe   cata**stroph**ic
7. **at**mosphere   atmo**spher**ic
8. a**nal**ysis   ana**lyt**ic
9. e**con**omy   eco**nom**ic
10. **me**teor   mete**or**ic
11. **per**iod   peri**od**ic
12. **id**iot   id**iot**ic